Resilient Hope:
Encountering the Unexpected

Elwin P. Ahu

Cover design by

Empowered Presentations

ISBN-13: 978-1540551191

DEDICATION

To Joy, Brandon and Jared who gave me a reason to live;
To the spiritual warriors of Metro Christian Church and
from around the world who gave me the strength to fight;
To my Lord and Savior Jesus Christ who gave me life.

Table of Contents

ACKNOWLEDGMENTS

"Your love has given me great joy and encouragement, because you, brother, have refreshed the hearts of the Lord's people."
(Philemon 1:7 NIV)

To the many who have encouraged me through the years to "write your book," because of your continuous support, you have refreshed my hearts.

- Metro Christian Church's council, for your stalwart leadership in the early years of our church;
- Metro's faithful volunteers committed to the Cause of Christ and strengthened in the face of adversity;
- Dr. Phil Suh, Dr. Jon Fukumoto – no better than you;
- Nursing staff of Queen's Medical Center; professionally competent, graciously caring;
- Prayer partners throughout the world;
- Copyeditors Kelli, Walt, Corinne and Nate; your skill and heart helped to shape this book into a more coherent and articulate book than I had written.

Finally, Brandon and Jared – you gave me the reason and will to live. To my precious, Joy, you stand taller in faith and deeper in love with Jesus than the depths of the sea. Thank you.

May you be refreshed in your soul.

–Elwin

Foreword

The year was 1990 - Home Alone was in theaters, Will Smith starred in a new show as the "Fresh Prince", and one of the greatest upsets in sports history was about to shock the world. The heavyweight champion of the boxing world, "Iron" Mike Tyson, was cutting down his challengers like a chainsaw in a chopstick factory and waltzed into the ring that night with a perfect 37-0 record. But James "Buster" Douglas stepped into the ring with something more powerful than a potent uppercut. In his corner was "resilient hope." It emboldened the challenger to encounter the impossible and in the tenth round, it was the challenger, Douglas, who overcame the odds and walked away as the champion.

Hope is a peculiar thing. Without it, we are buried under mountains of doubt, anger, cynicism, and unforgiveness. With it, our greatest obstacles are put in perspective, our focus shifts from problem to solution, and heavy weight champions of the world are suddenly beatable.

We all know someone who has hope, and we've all desperately needed it at pivotal times in our lives, especially when we encounter the unexpected. The funny thing about hope is that the only way to receive it, is to believe it. People can give us hope, but only if we allow them to. Inspiring stories abound in our digital culture, but unless we choose to believe the hope embedded in them, they simply remain reports of happenings. We must choose hope, lest it pass us by.

That's what I pray this book brings to your life: resilient hope. Hope that your situation, no matter how bleak, will get better. That the road may be long, the cliffs may be jagged, the tunnel may be dark, but there is a light at the end of it, ever so faintly beckoning us to believe that the flicker of a votive a mile away can be the evidence of better days ahead. Hope rises upward, and brings all that grasp onto her hand along for the ride.

How do I know this?

I have had the pleasure of a ringside seat to the battle that my dad fought with cancer. But as anyone who has sat in the first few rows of a title bout may attest, the closer you are, the bloodier it gets. And boy, did it get bloody. My dad has always been an athlete, taken care of himself, exercised and ate well. To me, he was nearly invincible. So to see him debilitated by the effects of leukemia was shocking. It was even harder to see him slip closer and closer to the dim doorstep of death. I remember being in his hospital room, when the mood was darker than the lighting, and hope seemed farther away than a warm day in winter. A frigid fear enveloped our family as we faced the possibility that we might actually lose him.

But it was then that a fighter needed to be coaxed to get up. It was either fight with every fiber, or throw in the towel. Win or go home. And my dad is a fighter. He might have been down, but not for the count. He was hard-pressed, but not crushed, knocked down, but not destroyed. What drove him? Resilient Hope. Hope that God wasn't done with him yet, that the call ahead of him was greater than the journey he had traveled thus far. Hope that he would be able to grow old with his beloved wife, see his youngest son graduate from high school, and play with his unborn future grandchildren. So he got up off the mat and started swinging.

Today, four years later, we were able to celebrate dad's 62nd birthday, my brother is one year away from starting high school, and my wife and I are expecting our first child. Looks like dad is going to be able to experience all of those things he was hoping for after all.

Hope is a powerful thing. Whoever or whatever is standing in the opposite corner of the ring that you find yourself in, I hope that you are encouraged by the story found in these pages to get up, keep swinging, and never throw in the towel.

- Brandon Q. Ahu

Introduction

In the beginning God created the heavens and
the earth. Now the earth was formless and empty,
darkness was over the surface of the deep,
and the Spirit of God was hovering over the waters.
(Genesis 1:1-2 NIV)

Every miracle begins with a problem. It's an axiom that can be traced back to the beginning, where the Book of Genesis recorded the initial core of creation as anything but organized and in perfect order. On the contrary, there was nothing but darkness and void, creation was "formless and empty;" in other words, there was a problem. But in the midst of the problem, there was God. And over the darkness and in the chaos, God's Spirit hovered and brought about a miracle . . . and God said it was good.

Are you willing to encounter the chaos, to face your problem in order to experience your miracle? Miracles have been abundant in my life, but no more profound than when our family experienced our "darkness" in the winter of 2012. Although I maintained a lifestyle of healthy habits and disciplines, nothing prepared us for what we were about to encounter. On Dec. 7, 2012, our family was rudely introduced to our problem. Its name: "Acute Promyelocytic Leukemia," a form of cancer that, like all others, has refused to discriminate against race, religion, gender or socio-economic status. For centuries it has meticulously maneuvered its way into the lives of millions of people, stealing their joy and eventually breath from their lungs.

Cancer is a thief. Every year, it robs thousands of lives. In 2015, according to the American Cancer Society, "about 589,430 Americans were expected to die of cancer, or about 1,620 people per day. Cancer is the second most common cause of death in the U.S., exceeded only by heart disease, and accounts for nearly one of every four deaths." (www.cancer.org).

But it's not just the life of the patient that cancer unapologetically rips away. Its unforgiving effects on the human body cheats a family from enjoying the life of their infected mom or dad, their son or daughter, brother or sister when it strikes at the heart of a home. It steals the promised love and lifetime companionship of a spouse, that once lost, never returns. But in the midst of the problem, a miracle awaits.

Miracles still happen today. They happen every day and are available to anyone, regardless of the person's belief in Jesus Christ or not, and hope stands at the corner of every street. I believe it with all my heart. It's when our eyes are open and our hearts are ready to receive that we will see and experience the miracles of God.

There are thousands of miracles to be experienced by every single one of us. But, just as a journey of 1,000 miles begins with a single step, so does the making of a miracle begin with a single problem.

In the Bible, every miracle began with a problem:

> Abraham was 99 years old when promised by God that he would be the father of many nations (Genesis 17:4).
>
> Moses and the Israelites faced a dead end at the Red Sea before God opened the door to their future (Exodus 14:21).
>
> Jesus faced death by crucifixion before the world witnessed the miracle of the resurrected power of God (Mark 16:6).

I've often said that I welcomed any challenge to live on the edge of life. It's on the edge where your attention is drawn to Jesus. Peter stood on the edge of the boat with his eyes focused upon the Lord, which allowed him to confidently step out of the boat and there, in the middle of a storm, he experienced the miracle of walking on water (Matthew 14:29).

I've wondered what the water felt like; probably uncomfortably cold, with a chilling breeze blowing into Peter's face. But his spirit was confident and stood in the midst of a storm with no guarantees that he would survive. Each new step toward Jesus never got any easier, as it took him, for all practical purposes, one step away from the perceived safety of the boat. But Peter kept walking. Each step presented its own set of problems, but each step also turned into its own set of miracles.

My diagnosis with cancer pushed me a bit closer to the edge than I would have wanted. Every day, each step that I took – together with my family in our fight against leukemia – revealed the working hands of God. But, we had to be willing to step into the problem in order to discover the miraculous that God was waiting to reveal.

Here's a prayer that I learned along this journey and would encourage anyone seeking the miracles of God to memorize and recite:

> *"Lord, give me eyes to see what You're seeing,*
> *Ears to hear what You're saying,*
> *And a heart that is open and willing to obey."*

It's when we possess the eyes to see, ears to hear, and a heart that welcomes the revelation of God's mighty works into our lives that we step into the miraculous with God. Without Him, miracles are overlooked as "just coincidental" or perceived as "just luck," and we disregard the mighty hand that had been at work all along.

The following pages are a compilation of my notes I recorded in "real time" during my hospitalization against leukemia. They capture the battle that I encountered along the journey; one that was filled with uncertainties, questions and doubts, frustrations and strain. But each step led me to renew my faith, trust and hope in the miraculous that's possible for anyone on a journey with God.

Making Sense of the Insensible

"Do not be anxious about anything, but in every situation, by prayer and petition, with thanksgiving, present your requests to God. And the peace of God, which transcends all understanding, will guard your hearts and your minds in Christ Jesus."
(Philippians 4:6-7 NIV)

December 7, 1941 holds a special place in history for America and the world. It will always be remembered as a day that we honor and commemorate the sacrifice of thousands of men and women of the Armed Services who lost their lives during the deliberate attack on Pearl Harbor and other military bases in Hawaii by the Japanese Imperial Forces. One act of war launched the United States into World War II. It was a day President Franklin D. Roosevelt declared as a "day that will live in infamy"[1] in the annals of history.

The "day that will live in infamy" for our family occurred exactly 71 years later on Dec. 7, 2012, but for a much different reason. It was the day cancer declared war on me. Not unlike the assault on Pearl Harbor, this "attack" had clandestinely crept into my life unannounced. There were no visible warning signs – there were no symptoms, no family medical history that would have alerted our family of the "enemy" that was lurking in my system, patiently waiting to wage against my body.

Cancer caught us off guard; it was totally unanticipated, and it left my family and me staring at the possibility of death. Nothing made any sense. But in the confusion and chaos, a hidden miracle was waiting to be revealed. We eventually recognized it in the working of God's hands that were wrapped around the diagnosis of the disease. No one could have imagined it.

---

[1] https://www.archives.gov/education/lessons/day-of-infamy/

Rewind the hourglass of time to the year 2006. My wife, Joy, and I had just adopted our son, Jared, from China. We were introduced to him during a church mission trip to the People's Republic in 2004. He was just 20 months old and recovering from a recent, radical, open-heart surgery that corrected a congenital heart defect. He was being cared for in a foster facility for children with medical challenges, and it was there where Joy fell in love with him.

Regardless of his frail condition, there was no doubt in Joy's mind: Jared was to be our son. Of all the children who resided at that facility, he was the only one who captured her heart. And considering China's strict adoption policies, it was a miracle that God blessed us with this one special child from a country composed of more than 1.4 billion people. Little did we realize how Jared's adoption would eventually be the key to the discovery of the cancer hidden within me.

Fast-forward time to Dec. 3, 2012. It was a picture-perfect day in paradise as Joy and I headed out the door for our routine walk. Our normal route typically covered about eight miles. On this particular morning, however, we intentionally added a stop at the doctor's office to pick up medicine for Jared. He was now a nine-year-old dealing with allergies. It was intended to be an impromptu in and out visit, since we were still in our walking cycle. But during our brief stopover, Jared's doctor asked if I would take a blood and lab test.

His random request surprised me. Why would my *child's* doctor ask his dad to take such an arbitrary test? Chance? Coincidence? As it turned out, it was anything but fortuitous. God had a reason; just as our adoption of Jared six years earlier had a purpose: to give me a reason to visit a doctor when I needed it most. As it turned out, timing meant everything.

Procrastination almost got the better of me. Urgency wasn't calling, as far as I knew. My aversion to needle pokes and the sight of blood, even if it's my own, also kept me from scheduling an immediate lab test. Moreover, historically, all my previous lab reports were uneventful and consistently documented a healthy body.

"So, what's the rush," I thought.

A couple of days had passed before I finally gave in to guilt and subjected myself to the lab. In hindsight, it was the best decision I ever made. The very next morning, less than 24 hours after my blood tests, Dr. Phil's office called and requested to see me as soon as possible.

"Why? What showed up on the exam," I wondered. *"Was my blood sugar too high? Am I vitamin deficient? Was it high cholesterol? Why the urgency?"*

I didn't have a clue. After all, there were no signs or symptoms of anything out of the ordinary in my health.

Joy and Jared accompanied me to the exam room that afternoon, expecting a quick report followed by a relaxing, pizza night as a family. When we arrived, Dr. Phil wasted no time. My lab tests revealed that I was infected with a rare form of leukemia known as "Acute Promyelocytic Leukemia (APL)." And, at that moment, no other words mattered, except "Leukemia."

It meant cancer, chemotherapy, nausea, vomiting, hair loss and baldness, and many other unknown effects. What seemed inevitable, however, were the roads that would eventually lead to death. Dr. Phil proceeded to explain the expected rapid deterioration of blood cells – red, white and platelets – the cause of the disease's unpredictable fatality rates.

Urgency was now calling. The doctor's staff had alerted the emergency room at a nearby hospital and secured an immediate appointment with one of Hawaii's top oncologists who specialized in hematology, diseases of the blood. All other specialists weren't available for another 30 days. The ER was expecting to receive me that night.

We left Dr. Phil's office, not quite sure what had just hit us. Our pizza night turned into the most awkward dinner our family ever experienced. No one talked; no one wanted to openly consider the perceived outcome that loomed on the horizon, as it does in all other leukemia cases. But our individual minds raced with a litany of "what if" questions:

"What if I never recover?"

"What if I die?"

"What if Jared grows up without a father?"

We headed home to prepare for our emergency room visit, not quite ready for what reality was about to reveal of my condition that had progressively deteriorated.

Once admitted to the ER, additional blood samples were drawn. Every report confirmed the truth: my overall condition had indeed worsened overnight. My rude awakening turned into a nightmare. It was especially daunting to hear how my platelets were now well below acceptable levels, a condition called "disseminated intravascular coagulation (DIC)"[2] sounding the alarm for the potential of spontaneous internal hemorrhaging and how unintentional bumps and bruises – if undetected and left untreated – could potentially cause me to bleed to death. The doctor's recommendation: immediate admission into the hospital with blood infusions to begin ASAP.

It was as if someone slammed a hammer into the center of my soul. I tried to hold on to my faith, to keep my spirits above the positive mark as I laid on the gurney in front of my wife and child. But it was difficult to watch as each updated detail of my declining state shredded their inner spirits. Emotionally, they were on a downhill free-fall. It felt as if we were all standing on the edge of death looking into the depths of a dark cavern of uncertainty ahead.

Questions and doubts flooded my mind in nano seconds, as I fought to keep my composure positive on the outside, but my insides were dying, literally and emotionally:

- *"Yes, I believed in the healing power of God, but ..."*

---

[2] https://www.nhlbi.nih.gov/health/health-topics/topics/dic

- *"I believe in faith and trust, but ..."*
- *"We just planted a new church in January. Why God, are You allowing me to be afflicted now?"*
- *"Am I being punished for the sins of my life? Is this retribution for my previous sins against You?"*

My eldest son, Brandon, a youthful 31-year-old, who had agreed to assist me with the start of our new church in the past six months, needed to be told of my condition. If I needed to remain hospitalized for 30 days, it meant missing our Christmas and New Year's services at church; it meant missing my birthday.

One phone call to Brandon and within minutes, he arrived at the ER. That night, he became every father's dream come true. After briefly discussing the short list of options, he bravely stood ready to take the reins of the church during my absence, with no questions or doubts. The ball needed to be handed off, and he was ready to run it down the field. He exhibited every ounce of confidence he could muster . . . but I knew, deep inside, he was a twisted mess of emotions as he witnessed his dad lie in a state of uncertainty. I always tried to be strong for him, but now in my weakness, he needed to find strength. My only assurance was the promise that the Lord would be with him.

Immediately, a flurry of medical attendants whisked me away to a private and restricted room where IV needles were meticulously inserted into my veins and began the infusion of necessary fluids and medications. Midnight had come and passed blindly by and the hour arrived when reality demanded that my family return home. It was probably one of the toughest separations we've ever had to work ourselves through, not knowing what the future held – the length of my absence from them, or my prognosis. Wrapped in our hugs were positive assurances we tried to force upon each other as we tried to stay strong, especially for Jared. But emotionally, we were being torn apart with each passing moment that led to our final good-byes.

There was just too much we experienced, received and needed to process in just a matter of a few hours that one day. We knew what had to be done, but the weight of uncertainty and the fear of the unknown were finally hitting the heart, like a boulder crushing our souls. Night turned into morning, one tick of the clock at a time. My only consolation was Joy's text messages to me in the early morning hours that reassured me of her love.

Uncertainty and the fear of the unknown will deflate even the strongest faith if you allow it to take residence in your mind and in your heart. We needed to stay strong, but the fear of the unknown heavily weighed upon our hearts. It turned out to be a long, long night. Frequent changes of tubes and transfusion bags, plus the routine intermittent monitoring of my blood pressure provided me with practically no sleep at all. In a few hours, the sun was going to shine again, but I wondered if it would shine again on me.

It's easy to explain faith in the circumstances of someone else's struggles, but when the rubber of faith meets the road of reality in your own life, how do you begin to make sense of the insensible? I've always believed in the promise of God's peace:

> *"Do not be anxious about anything, but in every situation, by prayer and petition, with thanksgiving, present your requests to God. And the peace of God, which transcends all understanding, will guard your hearts and your minds in Christ Jesus."*
>
> (Philippians 4:6-7 NIV)

"Help me, Lord; it's now time to live out what I believe," I prayed.

Seeing Beyond the Sorrow

"Weeping may last through the night,
but joy comes with the morning."
(Ps. 30:5 NLT)

Morning arrived; it was a brand new day. So, why did I feel like a wreck? Somehow, with faith, everything was supposed to be fine, right? After all, as a pastor of a church, a teacher of God's Word and an advocate of His promises, shouldn't all of this make sense? The night was over, but where was the joy that was supposed to meet me in the morning? If Jesus was my Healer and my Savior, then why were there still doubts that lingered in the recesses of my heart, taking residence in the voids left behind by hope that seemed to have slipped away overnight?

"Joy" certainly wasn't wrapped up in the details of the disease that we were to learn more about in the morning. The more we were told, the more it appeared as if God's once-reassuring hands were slowing fading out of reach.

"Acute promyelocytic leukemia," or "APL," a form of acute myeloid leukemia ("AML"), is a cancer of the blood-forming tissue found in the bone marrow. A normal-functioning bone marrow produces red blood cells (erythrocytes) that carry oxygen, white blood cells (leukocytes) that protect the body from infection, and platelets (thrombocytes) that are involved in blood clotting. In an APL patient, however, the abnormally functioning bone marrow accumulates immature white blood cells (promyelocytes) which, if left uncontrolled and untreated, develop into adolescent-like, rebellious and renegade cells, and lead to a reduction of normal white and red blood cells and platelets in the body. This results in the following symptoms:

- Susceptibility to bruising
- Appearance of small red dots (blood clots) under the skin

- Nosebleeds and bleeding from the gums
- Blood in the urine, or excessive menstrual bleeding

The reduction of red blood cells (anemia) also cause people with APL to appear pale in skin color, or experience excessive tiredness and fatigue from the lack of healthy, oxygen-rich blood. Further, the loss of normal white blood cells in individuals infected with APL cause patients to heal slowly from injuries or require them to fight more frequent battles against infections.[3] Historically, APL was considered to be one of the most fatal forms of acute leukemia, especially when diagnosed in older patients more than 55 years old,[4] with early death within 30 days of diagnosis, many times occurring from uncontrolled and untreated internal hemorrhaging.[5] I realized I was walking the thin line; my 58th birthday was in just 11 days.

There was the problem, in a nutshell. So, where was the miracle? It couldn't be seen in what our natural eyes saw or discovered in the logical dimensions of our world's reality. If there was indeed a miracle to be revealed, it would require us to look beyond the sorrow to recognize it. On the morning after, as Joy and I sat and reflected and tried to see through the depression and despondency of yesterday, two things began to emerge.

---

[3] https://ghr.nlm.nih.gov/condition/acute-promyelocytic-leukemia
[4] http://www.nature.com/bcj/journal/v5/n4/full/bcj201525a.html
[5] http://www.bloodjournal.org/content/118/5/1248

First, the frailty of my health called attention to the urgency to express our love for one another. We wholeheartedly agreed: our love between us should never remain silent and assumed. As we talked privately for the first time since the diagnosis, at times overcome with emotion, we realized how we had failed to consistently and faithfully express the degree of our love for one another. We vowed to never stop articulating our love for each other. It was a privilege that God had given us. However, neither of us knew when the reality of death would rudely interrupt our time together.

Sorting through the sorrow, we also began to see the handprint of God – His plans and intentions – that seemed buried in yesterday's encounter with chaos. Could it be that this was yet another step we were being asked to faithfully respond to? Would our hearts be prepared and ready to obey, yet again? Taking steps of faith with God wasn't unfamiliar to us:

- In January 2000, during the prime of my legal career, we truly believed a calling of God compelled me to walk away from the distinction of being a circuit judge for the State of Hawaii, to step down from the judicial bench without regrets or reservations, and faithfully step up to the throne of God, as I transitioned into full-time ministry;

- In March 2006, inspired once again to respond as God led us through the process, we adopted our son, Jared; not a problem for younger parents, but a major lifestyle detour for any couple whose combined age totaled 101 years (I won't say which one pushed us over the century mark);

- In January 2012, following God's direction again, as I stepped away from a secure staff role at a mega-church to begin a new church plant at 57 years "young."

In virtually every unimaginable opportunity in faith, each step we took placed us on a pathway that allowed us to experience the "joy" of seeing our faith perfected.

Isn't that God's desire for all of us? It was to perfect his faith that God compelled Abraham to walk the distance to sacrifice Isaac, only to reveal the "joy" of a sacrificial ram after Abraham's obedience. It was to perfect the faith of Moses when God commanded him to lead two million people to the edge of a raging Red Sea, only to reveal the "joy" of dry land as the sea parted for the people to cross. It was to perfect Peter's faith when the Lord called him to step out of the boat in the midst of a storm and revealed the "joy" of a pathway to walk upon water, as long as Peter remained focused on Him.

The perfection of our faith is God's greatest desire for our lives. He will oftentimes take the most difficult experience we encounter along life's journey and convert it to the most joyous, faith-perfecting miracle, if we choose to see through the sorrow and obediently walk toward the miracle.

We are encouraged "to consider it all joy when facing trials of many kinds," for the perfection of our faith (James 1:2). What launches us into the process of perfection is when we are willing to choose to see beyond the sorrow and not shy away from the seasonal setback or failure, challenge or encounter. It's when we choose to willingly engage the problem and faithfully obey. When we are willing to step into the process, weeping and trials may last through the dark shadows of the night, but the joy of a faith being perfected will certainly come in the morning . . . and Jesus will turn the whole process into another miracle. It's then that the Lord will open the door to a greater testimony.

From Pain to Peace

"The Lord is my light and my salvation,
whom shall I fear . . . of whom shall I be afraid?"
(Psalm 27:1 NIV)

Nothing else occupied my mind today, except the thought of having to undergo the dreaded bone marrow exam to confirm the initial diagnosis of "APL." It's designed as an intrusive procedure to retrieve samples of bone marrow, the spongy tissue inside my bones, that a lab could confirm or deny whether healthy, normal blood cells were being produced.[6]

As I lay prone on my hospital bed, the nurse began to prep and sterilize the area that surrounded the upper ridge of the back of my right hipbone, draping it with a surgical cloth to frame the examination site. A local anesthesia was administered to numb the area from pain that was to be expected from the initial incision. A probe was then inserted and guided by the doctor's trained hands. Its eventual destination: the surface of my bone. Then, while applying constant pressure, the doctor began to rhythmically push on the probe until the tip cracked through the brittle upper layer of my hipbone. It triggered an immediate burning sensation that permeated throughout my tissues, a feeling I will never forget.

I gripped firmly to my bed sheets, and with my jaws tightly clenched, I let out a deliberate and exhaustive groan, as I buried my face in my pillow and tried to hold my sanity from screaming inexplicable expletives aloud. It was the only buffer that stood between the puncture wound and my true expression of the excruciating torture of this exam.

---

[6] http://www.mayoclinic.org/tests-procedures/bone-marrow-biopsy/basics/

Then, it got worse. It was time to withdraw the liquefied marrow from the bone. The doctor warned me to brace myself and, as if on cue, I began to recite every Scripture verse that I had memorized, from Genesis to Revelation. I pressed into the assurances of God and searched for His promised peace in Philippians 4, but nothing could minimize the sharp and unbearable sting that began to radiate throughout my entire body as the doctor slowly and methodically withdrew the marrow's fluid into the syringe.

I was a believer in Christ, I've contended for His healing power in other patients, I've called out for His peace to rescue broken homes and shattered lives, but nothing could silence the piercing reality of what I was called upon to experience. Instinctively, I began searching for worship songs, biblical verses and prayed for the Holy Spirit's intervention. But, they all seemed to be overruled by the intensity of the stinging that emanated from the point of penetration. The aspiration took just a few minutes, but it felt like an eternity to me.

But, it was then that my thoughts immediately raced to the cross of Jesus. I could only imagine the pain the Lord must have experienced as He laid on the rugged, knotted wooden beam with arms extended and palms forcefully opened to receive the rusted spikes that were driven into His hands and feet by the Roman soldiers. As I thought of what must have overwhelmed Him, His pain became my only source of comfort knowing that the aggregate of my sufferings paled in comparison to what Jesus experienced on the cross. My own reality reminded me that Jesus subjected Himself, not because of an illness that demanded a blood smear for a lab test, nor because of a penalty that needed to be paid. Instead, He laid Himself out for no other reason than to demonstrate His love for us.

> *"But he was pierced for our transgressions, He was crushed for our iniquities; the punishment that brought us peace was on Him, and by His wounds we are healed"* (Isaiah 53:5 NIV).

He was the Son of God, the Messiah and the Anointed One, but He, too, felt the reality of pain. And He did it for us. Regardless of how undeserving we are of His love and forgiveness, He was willing to sacrifice His life for each of us. As I laid there in my anguish, I realized how much more He bore on the cross for me. If my Lord could suffer for me, then I could certainly bear through the reality of my own suffering, regardless of the weight of the pain that l was required to accept for the moment. In that moment of remembrance, I saw my pain juxtaposed against His and the reason He did it for me . . . and in that moment of pain, I found my peace.

Lab tests confirmed what everyone initially feared. After reviewing the bone marrow samples, pathologists determined that 95 percent of my marrow was occupied by abnormal cells. In other words, I was severely infected. By all indications, I was a walking dead man. I shouldn't have been alive. The cancerous cells were destroying all my healthy red and white blood cells and platelets. My marrow wasn't functioning normally. It reproduced nothing but new adolescent renegade cells running rampant throughout my system.

The textbooks were all in agreement; the doctors had no doubts. I should have been severely anemic, totally fatigued and unable to function fully as a person. Exhaustion should have laid me flat on my back. Severe bleeding should have been detected along the gum lines of my mouth and within my nasal cavities. The low platelet counts made me highly vulnerable to the risk of spontaneous abdominal bleeding. The lack of white cells left me with a deficient immune system and unprepared to defend against the viruses and infections from everyday bacteria.

With such news of gloom, where was the miracle? It wouldn't be found in the pain of the "here and now," but could only be seen if we were willing to look beyond the present. We needed eyes to see, ears to hear and a heart that was open and willing to obey. And with such eyes and ears, and a willing heart, this is what I discovered, even in the pain of the present: God had been at work long before the pain. His hand had prepared a miracle for me to see, but I needed to experience the pain to realize it. More importantly, I needed to develop a heart that was prepared to receive it.

> *"Lord, give me eyes to see what You're seeing,*
> *Ears to hear what You're saying,*
> *And a heart that is open and willing to obey."*

When I began to trace the workings of God's hands, I discovered a "string" that tied my present pain to our obedience of the past. Therein lied the miracle for the day:

- By following God's call to step off the judicial bench and step into full time ministry, Joy and I were able to travel on a mission to China;

- Our mission trip to China introduced Joy to Jared, which led to his adoption into our family;
- Jared's adoption led us to visit *his doctor* where he "randomly" asked for a blood test that eventually led to the diagnosis of my condition;
- Had I delayed the hospital admission, my condition would have remained untreated and you would be reading my obituary, rather than this book.

With eyes to see what He sees, it gave me confidence to know that God was always at work, before and even through the pain. And, He's still at work today. So, as I prepared myself for the dreaded chemotherapy to begin, with all its related difficulties, complications, nausea and discomfort, I found rest in the peace of God. I was confident to be able to bear yet another segment of my journey with a peace that only He could have provided, knowing that regardless how painful the road may get, I was assured of the promise of peace that I would find in Him.

Faith to Move Forward

"Now faith is confidence in what we hope for and assurance about what we do not see."
(Hebrews 11:1 NIV)

Just when you think you have your own set of problems, isn't it just like God to show you something beyond your own suffering that calls attention to the blessings you already have?

Spending 24 hours in a hospital room can be suffocating. As Joy and I ventured to the outside lanai to grab a breath of fresh air and to remind ourselves that life still exists outside the hospital walls, we saw a patient too young to have to suffer from this vicious and venomous disease. No one deserves to suffer, especially those who haven't had a chance to live. She was admitted to the cancer critical care unit four months earlier and had hoped to beat an abdominal cancer. But the tangled strands of feeding tubes and IV lines connected to machines attached to her young body told the story of an anticipated bitter end. She was unable to eat and slowly deteriorated under the stranglehold of cancerous cells that seemed to methodically steal the life God gave her.

My hospital "neighbor" was another example of the prolonged battles cancer demands from its victims. When I arrived, she had already been a patient for 71 days. Although her treatment intensified over time and took her on journeys to Seattle and other mainland cities to seek a cure, she never recovered. The list of patients goes on. Space doesn't permit me to provide a fair description of each patient's unique journey in his or her battle against cancer's advances.

Such is the fragility of life. No one aspires to suffer. Life wasn't meant to live cooped up behind four walls, attached to machines that monitor blood pressures, heart beats, fluids, feeding tubes and needle pokes. But, it's in the midst of suffering – when life comes to a sudden and abrupt stop – at the intersection of hope and hopelessness, that one's faith is tested.

Hebrews 11:1 defines faith as the "confidence in what we hope for and assurance about what we do not see;" quite simple and straightforward when we find ourselves living a life of no concerns. However, when we're called upon to suffer and are forced to live within the darkened hallways of the unknown, or under the shadows of uncertainty, our faith challenges us to ask:

- "In what do we have confidence?"
- "For what do we hope?"
- "What are we assured of that we do not see?"

Therein defines a degree of faith that will move us forward. We'll always move toward what we choose to place our faith in.

In the midst of uncertainty, we're naturally inclined to gravitate toward life's "guarantees." No one likes to fail or to come up short. No one celebrates a loss or a season of suffering, and so we pursue the best possible means to avoid defeat, regardless of the costs. We'll lean in the direction of the high- percentage, low-to-no risk opportunities. We'll favor the side of life that's supported by positive statistics. We'll search for the proverbial "path of least resistance" to reach a desired end that we've defined for ourselves.

But, in the pursuit of our self-defined destinations, we risk forfeiting the plans that God may have appointed for our future. When our perception is that God's way will only point us to the negative, painful, fearful side of the statistical scale – when His plans fail to agree with our plans – our faith fades. Our confidence is shaken; we lose hope.

For example, every patient stricken with cancer wants to be healed. But what happens to our testimony of faith when healing is delayed or when prayers go unanswered? To which side of the scale will we allow our hope to slide? What if suffering increases, rather than subsides, or if reality demands that life be lived in the shattered dreams and the pain of the "here and now?" Will faith still be anchored to a confidence and an assurance in the power of God? Will hope still prevail?

If our desire is to move forward, then there really is no other choice when one's mortality rests in the balance, weighted by the uncertainties and the unexpected that life delivers. There is no other choice than to secure one's faith – our hope, confidence and assurances – in a God who knows what's best, even if we can't make sense of it all. From the vantage point of my faith, I felt empowered daily to press through the difficulties that confronted me.

The frailty of our mortality is a certainty in this life. No one knows which statistical category we will eventually slip into at the end of the road. Medical journals may outline the percentages of one patient being healed over another or paint a positive picture of a 90 percent cure rate for the "lucky" ones. What about the 10 percent who fail the test and are not restored to wholeness or granted the gift of another day? To what do they attach their confidence and assurances? Where does their hope come from? No one knows what exactly what will happen to anyone's eventual destiny, not even doctors. No one knows .

. . except God.

Therefore, throughout my journey, I chose to define my faith not by the statistical cure rate of this disease. My confidence and assurance rested in the belief that, no matter the outcome of my present sufferings – whether my body responded positively to the treatment or not; whether I was granted to fall on the statistical side of recovery or not; that through the misery I was called upon to bear, God knew full well the plans that He had for my life (Jeremiah 29:11). I was confident and assured, and I pressed toward the goal – that God's Word would be preached and the reality of the Kingdom would come alive to an even greater degree than it did before my affliction! He would shape my mess into His message. He would take the test that I was called upon to tackle and would turn it into His testimony of goodness and of His healing powers to be declared. Lives would change through this ordeal and faith levels will increase exceedingly beyond measure, and miracles – yes, life is full of them – would become a reality and celebrated.

Listen to what I wrote in the pages of the daily journal I kept:

> *Today, yet another miracle is waiting to happen – my next chemo treatment and another round of expected side effects stand ready to challenge me once more. The negative consequences are listed and they've been explained to me, but they won't be what I hope for. My confidence will remain in the Lord, in His healing, in the power of His restoration, and in the prayers that are being lifted up by so many saints around the world. Here we go again; two treatments down, two more to go. Strap on your seatbelts.*

Built on the Rock

"Therefore everyone who hears these words of mine and puts them into practice is like a wise man who built his house on the rock. The rain came down, the streams rose, and the winds blew and beat against that house; yet it did not fall, because it had its foundation on the rock."
(Matthew 7:24-25 NIV)

Some storms are predictable and easy to track, especially when using the latest in satellite technology. Others aren't. Some are but a passing shower; others leave an indelible mark in history and are best remembered for a devastating swath of destruction left behind. Such was the unwelcomed storm named "Leukemia" that thundered into our household. No one saw it coming. It struck hard and fast. The key to surviving the storm: rest on the rock of Jesus Christ. Though surprised, our family weathered the storm and today stands stronger physically, emotionally and spiritually, despite the waves of doubt, fear and uncertainty that had once swept over us.

Similar to all cancer cases, leukemia targeted more than just me, the patient. Its trials also tested my wife, as Joy expressed in her journal that chronicled her walk through the storm.

> *It was Friday, December 7, 2012, a day I will never forget and it's not because of Pearl Harbor. It started off being a normal Friday until Elwin came home. It was unusually early. The plan was to go to the doctor's with him, then go for an early dinner. I totally agreed, after all, that meant I didn't have to cook.*
>
> *Of course, we tried to think of reasons as to why it was so urgent for him to see the doctor. He wasn't sick or had any weird or unusual symptoms. We had no clue as to what we were about to hear.*
>
> *When Dr. Phil walked into the room, I remember him saying, "Okay, you're all sitting down," as if he had some alarming news to report to us. He started to explain the condition Elwin had, and I couldn't believe what I was hearing. We were told he had a rare*

form of leukemia called Acute Promyelocytic Leukemia (APL), cancer of the blood-forming tissue (bone marrow). There are more children, young adults or elderly that get it. He explained that while most illnesses would gradually worsen, not this one. It would start off gradual, but spike up at any time and once it spiked up, it would be fatal. What they didn't know was where exactly Elwin was on that scale.

While we were talking to the doctor, I kept thinking, "It's all a mistake! There was a blood mix-up! He's not sick, he's healthy; we exercise a lot and eat somewhat healthily." I was in denial.

Dr. Phil did all he could to help us through this ordeal, but he and the resident pathologist knew how urgent this situation was and made all the arrangements for admission to the emergency room. Time was of the essence. Elwin asked if we could have dinner before going to the ER and we were given the okay. We sat in silence through dinner, all in our own thoughts of what just transpired. "This couldn't be happening! Could we go and get a second opinion?" I thought. I don't really remember what we ordered for dinner.

After dinner, we headed for home. Jared needed to take a bath and I wanted to grab my Bible, another book, water, jacket and whatever else I thought we/I might need, expecting a long night in the ER.

Once we got there, Elwin was ushered into a screening room with glass walls. Jared kept walking up to the room, peering in and would inform me as to what was happening in there. He'd come back and say, "Dad has a mask on!" Then he would check again and say, "Dad had to put gloves on, too!"

It wasn't too long before they had us in a room and all of us were donned in masks, too. They took blood samples and didn't explain much to us as they scurried around to do what was necessary. We were later ushered into another room that was totally enclosed for isolation purposes. Most of the rooms just have curtains for privacy, but Elwin had to be in total isolation due to his neutropenia condition.[7]

Once the blood test results were examined, the ER doctor told us Elwin had to be admitted into the hospital for 30 days. But of course, Elwin asked how soon did he have to check in and if he could postpone it until a later date. I know he was thinking about the upcoming Sunday's message (since this was Friday evening) and not to mention his birthday, Christmas Eve, Christmas, New Year's Eve and New Hope Metro's 1st Anniversary in January. We were told he could bleed internally without knowing it if he were to bump something accidentally or fall. It seemed like there was no way out of being admitted into the hospital that night. Before giving them an answer, he asked if he could call his son.

Brandon came and everything was explained to him. Brandon was fully supportive and was more than willing to step in to do whatever was necessary to help his dad. That is a miracle. We know that Brandon would never have agreed, had he still been away. The Lord had brought Brandon to Metro just at the right time. Praise the Lord!

---

[7] Patients are diagnosed with "neutropenia" when there is a low level of neutrophils, a type of white blood cell, subjecting the individual to higher risk of developing serious infection. www.cancer.net/navigating-cancer-care/side-effects/neutropenia

Once that was settled, Elwin's journey began. We stayed until he was admitted into the hospital and settled in a room. By then it was after 11 p.m. and all I could think of was to get Jared home and in bed.

Jared had a long, heart-wrenching and exhausting day. Once I got him in bed, he began to cry again, just as he did in the ER. But this time he asked, "Is daddy going to die?" something I'm sure he thought of every time he cried in the ER. That was one question I didn't want to think of for fear of it coming true!

"No, don't say that," I responded, and as I talked to him, it was like I was convincing not only him, but me too! "Dad's not going to die, he's going to be okay! That's why he's in the hospital. The doctors are going to take real good care of him."

I explained to him that we need to put our trust in Christ and that there may be a time when he might really need me and I may not be there for him and there may be a time when he may really need his dad and for whatever reason, he may not be there for him. But, there is one person who would always be there for him no matter what, and that was Jesus Christ. He could call upon the Name of Jesus and Jesus would be there!

After we talked, I prayed for Jared, Elwin's situation and for our family. He was totally comforted and in better spirits when he went to bed. Praise the Lord!

Now, it was my turn. After a much needed hot shower and as I laid in bed, I started to recap everything that has just transpired. I know the doctor said, "If there is any cancer to have, this is the one to get for it is 95 percent curable." "But," I thought, "what about the other five percent?" That's excellent odds if you're guaranteed to be on the 95 percent side, but right now the five percent was equally as real. I didn't know what end of the spectrum Elwin was on. Then I realized time was of the essence and I was running out of time. I felt like I hadn't told Elwin, "I love you" enough. Did he even know how much I really love him? Had I done enough to show him how much I love him.

All these thoughts made me cry. Would I ever be able to prove my love for him, in the time we had left to share.

Fear started to envelope me, and all of a sudden, the house seemed quieter and darker and the bed felt bigger and empty, too! I cried, "Lord, I am so afraid, I don't want to be alone. Who's going to be lying next to me every night? Who's going to help me raise Jared? Who's going to be standing next to me when Jared graduates? Who's going to catch the lizard in the house for me? Who's going to change the light bulb when it goes out? Who's going to take my car in for servicing?"

In the midst of my fears and crying out to Him, I heard the Lord say, "I AM!"

And in that moment I knew He was going to be there for me. He has never left me nor forsaken me, and I knew I had nothing to fear. I can't explain it, but total peace washed over me and my thought process changed from one of fear to one of hope.

"Lord, I know You didn't take my husband out of the marketplace and into full-time ministry for nothing! You didn't take us to China, only to adopt a child in our old age for nothing! You didn't allow me to quit work with only 18 more months before qualifying to retire

with full benefits for nothing! You didn't allow us to leave our church and start a new one at an age where most people contemplate retiring to pioneer New Hope Metro for nothing!

I knew He wasn't done with us yet and I was filled with His hope and the future He had set for us.

God is my Lord and Savior, my Redeemer, my Helper, my Hope, my Strength, my Provider, my source of Joy, my Prince of Peace. He is trustworthy, He is faithful and true and He is the solid Rock that I stand on!

As we faced the winds of fear and doubt, we found our family's faith anchored to God's Word. It became the foundational pin that held us in place, regardless the challenges that were still ahead. As we confidently rested upon God's Word, it dried away our tears, calmed our shaken spirits, filled the voids of loneliness and gave us a renewed sense of hope each morning. I honestly don't know what we would have done without having Jesus as the Rock of our foundation of faith.

> *"Delight yourself in the Lord; and He will give you the desires of your heart"* (Psalm 37:4 NASB).

The miracle of the day: so far, I responded quite well to the chemo. There were minor bouts with nausea and headaches during the night, but they were within a manageable range of discomfort. My blood tests also began to show promise, so rather than providing blood samples twice a day, it was reduced to one sample per day. What a relief it was; no longer would I be considered the withdrawal window at the blood bank.

Hospitals have a unique way of reminding us of the unpredictable frailty of life. What a new baby brings into the world, cancer tries to steal. However, if our foundation is built on the Lord, His promises allow us to witness yet another miracle. I will be forever grateful to the Father for a brand-new day that now had new meaning. I survived the night and it was a blessing that I will never forget.

Defeating Doubt

"Trust in the Lord with all your heart and lean not on your own understanding; in all your ways submit to him, and he will make your paths straight."
(Prov. 3:5-6 NIV)

Nighttime has become my least favorite friend. It's the time nurses change shifts and everyone heads home or out to dinner, or to the movies, or to be any place but at the hospital. It's when visiting hours are declared over and Joy and Jared must return home . . . to our home. And I'm left in the quiet.

It's been a week since I was admitted to the hospital; a *looong* week that turned my world inside out and upside down. Each night was filled with one interruption followed by another: countless and frequent, hourly bathroom visits; bouts with nausea and intermittent throbbing headaches caused by the chemotherapy, while trying to keep myself from being tangled in the web of IV tubes as I tossed and turned during the night.

So this particular morning, like every morning since my admission, I looked forward to the arrival of daybreak, the sunrise, and Joy's visit. Although the sun strained to peer through the buildings and into my room each day, it was Joy's face that I looked forward to seeing. Every day, she faithfully stayed at my bedside, whether it was to watch TV, read her Bible or her book, catch up on the latest news in the daily paper or challenge her mind in a "*Sudoku*" puzzle. An exchange of words weren't necessary to feel her companionship. Conversation was good, but simply being in the presence of the one that I loved filled my emptiness each day. Today took a different twist.

As predicted by the doctors, my energy levels plummeted as the chemo raced throughout my body, indiscriminately killing the bad and good cells in my system. It was to be anticipated. This particular morning was no exception. I awoke and noticed a significant depletion in my energy levels and knew it would progressively deteriorate as the cumulative effect of the chemo treatments began to take its toll. It left me feeling awful, sickly, nauseated and lousy. I felt hopelessly pathetic.

It was Joy's phone call later that morning that seemed to suck the only breath of hope left from my day. She woke up with symptoms of a head cold. At any other time, it wouldn't have been a big deal, but my chemo treatment made me highly susceptibility to any colds, viruses and bacterial infections. Therefore, Joy wasn't able to visit me until her condition cleared, and neither could Jared. It wasn't the kind of morning I had expected. It meant my days would be spent alone, without knowing when she would be able to join me again. My neutropenia prohibited visitors and Joy was my only company. Now there was no one; only the sounds of beeping monitors filled the air.

It wasn't the only matter that complicated the day. Another issue developed that fueled more frustrations and began to test my faith once again. Compounded with the leukemia, CT scans revealed a "shadow" on my lungs that was producing an irritating, persistent cough. Was it a further indication of cancer now invading my lungs? Was it another kind of disease prompted by a weak immune system that was set to destroy more of my tissues? Its place of origin was unclear, considering I had travelled to foreign countries on mission trips in the past few years: China, Japan, Sierra Leone, El Salvador, all in the name of Christ and for God's purposes. I never expected to contract anything that would eventually harm me. After all, "God wouldn't allow me to be afflicted if I was doing His work . . . if I was doing good, right?" I reasoned.

Because of chemo's propensity to kill all of my blood cells – including the healthy white blood cells – slowly with each additional chemo treatment, I was left essentially immune deficient to any disease. Therefore, an additional healthcare professional was added to the team: a doctor who specializes in contagious and infectious diseases. He immediately ordered a round of multiple antibiotic infusions. Joy was no longer my bedside companion. Instead, I was left with hanging bags of saline, antibiotics, and blood transfusions who stayed with me throughout the day and night.

Have you ever had days when you just wanted to cry out to the Lord, "Now what?" Doubt can become a dangerous and suppressing tool of the enemy. When the unanticipated happens, and when hope flees, and all you can ask is, "Now what?" where do you turn to reset things back to a state of normalcy? The answer: God's Word, but not just the recitation of God's Word. There must be a receptivity to His Word, a willingness to consume, digest and convert His Word, and the promises He brings into the depth of your soul. Otherwise, we miss the miraculous healing power, the soothing comfort that only His Holy Spirit can bring.

In the frustrations of my day, I found myself meditating and consuming God's assurances of Isaiah 43:1-3 that was sent to me, paraphrased by a dear sister, Wanda, to personalize His Word in order to restore hope to my heart.

"But now, thus says The Lord who created you:
"Fear not, for I have redeemed you *Elwin*;
I have called you by your name *Elwin*
You are Mine.
When you pass thru the waters
I will be with you *Elwin*
When you walk thru the fire
You shall not be burned *Elwin*
Nor shall the flame scorch you *Elwin*
For I AM The Lord your God
The Holy One of Israel, your Savior, *Elwin*!"

This was exactly what I needed to believe. Despite the number of setbacks I would eventually face along this journey, I could confidently rest in the promise that I would not be harmed, that God still had full control over it all.
Proverbs 3:5-6 (NIV) has become our family's life verse:

> *"Trust in the Lord with all your heart, lean not on your own understanding."*

I've read it. I've memorized it. Now, I had to live it.

Conversation with God

"I wait for the Lord, my whole being waits,
and in His word I put my hope."
(Psalm 130:5 NIV)

It was yet another uncomfortable, unpleasant and annoyingly long night. My body wasn't feeling right; my mind was preoccupied with 1,000 questions and I was exhausted from the medications' side effects. War had been declared against the bands of rebellious and renegade cancer cells in my system and the battle was unrelenting. But the greater fight wasn't just a battle against my physical health. Despair desperately wrestled with my heart and made every effort to rob me of the last bits of hope onto which I frantically tried to cling.

Despondency and hopelessness made the hours of the night an unbearable wait. Even with the promise of the morning being just a few hours away, I wasn't looking forward to it. And in the frustrations of my moment, I began to contend with God.

"Why, Lord; why me," I asked in desperation, fearful of what His answer might be. Unknowingly and unintentionally, the "seeds of hopelessness" were being sown in my spirit and my frustrations fertilized its roots.

It was in those times that my conversations with God became authentically real. Walking with God wasn't new for me. As a pastor of a wonderful church, I had already experienced amazing God-sized miracles in the life of our church.

But in this moment, there were 1,000 additional questions I had ready and aimed at God regardless of what His answers might be:

> *"How much longer would I be in this hospital?"*
>
> *"Didn't I give You my life, and is this how I get rewarded?"*
>
> *"What will happen to my future? Will I ever live a normal life again?"*

With every question that I fired at God in rapid sequence, I constantly found myself circling back to the basic query: "Why me? Why now?"

And in the dark of the night, I clearly heard, "Because I'm preparing you." It wasn't an audible human voice; yet, I knew within my spirit it was the Lord.

"Preparing me for what?" I probed.

"Preparing you for heaven," He assured me.

"But I'm not ready," I reluctantly admitted.

"I know," said the Lord, as I then encountered the most profound moment of my spiritual walk with Him:

> *"I know, and that's why this journey is yours to take – so that you may know what it means to completely trust Me. It's having "pure trust." In heaven, there is only a complete trust in Me and in nothing else. After all, if you can't completely trust Me in heaven, whom will you trust when you're there? You will learn that degree of trust here on earth, as it is in heaven, but it can only be learned when you come face to face with adversity wrapped in the unthinkable and the undesirable. Only when you're willing to walk through the valley of the shadow of*

death and fear no evil, will you be in a position of complete trust."

"Are you taking me tonight?" I hesitantly wondered out loud. I really didn't want to know.

"No," came His reply, "but I want you to learn what "pure trust" is all about; then, I want you to teach others about it."

Did you catch that? In heaven there's only "pure trust," a complete trust that we must learn here on earth, as it will be in heaven. And the best tutor of trust is a teacher named "Adversity." We enroll in her class whenever we come face to face with hardship and confrontations that challenge our sense of hope. Every encounter with adversity has a purpose, not for our calamity, but to place us on the pathway that develop in us an authentic and genuine trust in the Lord. Walking through the valley of the shadow of death isn't supposed to be a death march for our soul, but a passageway that leads us to a place of complete and pure trust in Him, if we choose to take it.

Life's unfortunate and untimely events are our best tutors to teach us about the power present in God's Word. When the going gets tough and our confidence is challenged, the abstract promises of God are tested against the realities of unfairness found on the road of life. It's when we push ourselves to confront the inequities of our existence that we get to witness God's healing power and how His hope and peace come alive in living color.

When our desire, however, is to live a life without incident, peaceful and predictable, or when we constantly search for the onramp to the road of least resistance, I wonder how poorer we become by forfeiting the lessons that would have strengthened us for the journey ahead.

Without a doubt, this journey has tried and tested my faith. But the Lord is my Shepherd and I shall not want. Regardless of my sufferings, it paled in comparison to the crown He's reserved for the faithful who completely trust in Him. What I lack, He would surely provide in the "green pastures" and "quiet waters" of heaven. The Lord restores my soul.

This is an excerpt I wrote in my hospital journal:

> *Even though my journey has taken me through the valley where I've walked under death's shadow, I will not fear, for He is with me. He protects and comforts me, and His goodness will follow me all the remaining days of my life. And I will truly dwell in the Father's house forever and ever and ever.*
>
> *The power resident in His Word is real to me, as is the hope and peace that it brings. By trusting in Him, I'm prepared for the miracle He's about to reveal to me. My miracle for the day: I finished receiving my fourth and final chemo treatment! Now, I must be content to wait and trust in God's complete healing and the restoration of His strength.*

"Do you not know? Have you not heard? The Lord is the everlasting God, the Creator of the ends of the earth. He will not grow tired or weary, and his understanding no one can fathom. He gives strength to the weary and increases the power of the weak. Even youths grow tired and weary, and young men stumble and fall; but those who hope in the Lord will renew their strength. They will soar on wings like eagles; they will run and not grow weary, they will walk and not be faint."

(Isaiah 40:28-31)

When God Hits Reset

"And we know that in all things God works for the good of those who love him, who have been called according to his purpose."
(Romans 8:28 NIV)

Embarrassment and shame were my alarm clocks today. The accumulation of medications had reached its tipping point in me and my body reacted. My sheets were soiled and my clothes needed to be changed; needless to say, I was utterly humiliated. It proved to be the beginning of many other episodes that summoned the nursing staff to my "rescue" as I laid there draped in disgrace. But even in the midst of the day's discomfort and in my loss of dignity, there was still a miracle waiting to be realized.

It arrived when the doctor ordered the removal of my IV lines. They tied me to monitors like handcuffs and shadowed me everywhere I went, as if to haunt me through the hallways or to my frequent bathroom visits, day and night, lights glowing, beeping annoyingly calling attention to itself throughout the night. Uninterrupted sleep was impossible as I found myself fighting the tangled web of tubes each night. But, today I was free at last. Thank God Almighty, free at last!!

This "freedom" might seem small and meaningless to the rest of the world, but I saw it as a miracle. Being free reminded me how we often fail to appreciate the simple things in life, until it's taken from us. Perhaps it was God's way of hitting "Reset" to remind me of the importance to not take His blessings for granted. The entire ordeal of being tied to tubes and poked with needles molded a deeper appreciation within me for what we so often overlook: life's simple blessings.

I developed a sincere appreciation to simply sit with the one that I love, to have her with me throughout the day without any special reason, except to express the common bond we shared with one another. I felt blessed to be alive and to breathe one more breath to enjoy "borrowed time" with Joy, even if it was but for one more second. Each new morning when she arrived at my bedside simply meant I had been granted another chance to fall in love with her again and to appreciate the blessing that she has been to me. Joy was a gift directly from the Lord, and I was its recipient, only by His grace.

I came to appreciate my children with a deeper sense of love that I would have missed had God not hit "Reset." I began to see my son Brandon through new eyes, not only as a leader who was progressively developing into a leader's leader and able to communicate God's Word. I also appreciated his genuine love for God's people. And notwithstanding all the honors and accolades that will eventually come his way, I love him simply as my child whom I will love to the day I die, with a love that overflows from the heart of a father; a love and respect that will increase unconditionally with each new day.

And there's Jared ... What more can I say about a blessing from the heart of God? Active and rascal, he represents the fullness of life and how it should be lived and enjoyed. This ordeal has been tough on our little guy, who expressively feared the loss of his dad, but somehow, he found a way to redirect his fears into trust. Through this process, I proudly watched how he had grown with God and believed with a simple, child-like faith that his God would heal his dad.

Perhaps when God hits "Reset," His desire is to wash away the worthless, in order to replace it with the precious. He promised to faithfully stand poised and ready to work all things "*for the good of those who love him* (Romans 8:28 NIV)." How often do we run from having our lives "Reset" and instead look to escape the encounters that challenge our faith, and in doing so, we unknowingly trade the precious for the worthless. It especially happens in the chapters of life that we're unprepared to read when we're pressed and compelled to step into events that seem senseless, that make life more confusing and complex than what we expected.

Many times God hits "Reset" in the seasons of pain and discomfort, embarrassment and shame, or fear and frustration to catch our attention so we wouldn't miss the lessons we would have otherwise overlooked.

But therein lies the challenge for us: how much of our lives are we willing to allow God to reset in order to point us in the right direction? Life was expected to get worse for me before it would get better. As chemo's "poison" continued to work throughout my body, it progressively and indiscriminately destroyed the old cancerous cells, as well as my good and healthy cells. Doctors predicted that I would soon "hit the wall" and my strength would be totally depleted. The worst news of all – according to percentages, hair loss was an inevitable reality; my surroundings would soon serve as a depository for hair strands that would free-fall from my head. In the grander picture, my body was in "Reset" mode. It was the only way to get rid of the old in order to welcome the new. Physically, "Reset" meant a regeneration of new healthy cells that would – hopefully – carry me across the finish line.

In a similar way, when God hit "Reset" in my life, it tore away the old blindfold that hid my appreciation for the precious people, time, and relationships I already had. Although I waited, watched, hoped and prayed for relief from the pain and discomfort while still confined in my room, there was no better way to begin a new year of living. God is indeed faithful and just to turn all things for good to reset my life to be refreshed and renewed so I wouldn't miss what mattered most.

> *"[The Lord] has given us great and precious promises. These are the promises that enable you to share his divine nature and escape the world's corruption caused by human desires"* (2 Peter 1:4 NLT).

Encouragement – Medicine for the Soul

"Therefore encourage one another and build each other up, just as in fact you are doing."
(1 Thessalonians 5:11)

The best birthday gift I've ever received was unwrapped for me today. No, it wasn't in the form of new car, or an all expenses-paid trip to New York City, or a newly renovated dream kitchen and bathroom, although any of these would be nice! Confinement to a hospital room has a way of rearranging one's priorities. Of all the gifts that could ever be given, the best I received was this: *God filled my lungs and allowed me to live and breathe for yet another day.* After tiptoeing close to the edge of life's perimeter, I've come to appreciate the value of each new day and the breath of life He provides, by His grace.

I also received another gift of equal value: *prayers of encouragement from family and friends, at just the right moment, with just the right words to lift my fallen spirits.* Prayer is a powerful weapon, no doubt. And I know that if it weren't for the world-wide prayers of the saints, Joy and I wouldn't have possessed the inner strength to press through those awful moments of despair. Faith would have given way to fear and we would have sidestepped the sequence of lessons God intended for us to experience in order to enrich our lives.

Just as prayer is powerful, I believe encouragement is medicine for the spiritually depleted soul. Words that uplift, Scriptural promise of hope and healing, and even a light-hearted prompting refuel the soul like nothing else. I was blessed with this medicinal dose exactly when I needed it most.

Truthfully, it turned out to be another rough night for me. It was the eve of my birthday, I was free from my IV and expected to sleep through the night, undisturbed. But, it wasn't to be. The sleep-stealer this time: a dry, hacking and persistent cough that somehow developed overnight. I was told it was to be expected since the chemo would destroy my white blood cells, lowering my immunity against viral or bacterial infections.

Chemo also destroyed the red blood cells that carried oxygen throughout the body; thus, at some point I would "hit the wall," fatigued and exhausted. I guess, as timing would have it no other way, all of the above had to happen in unison on the morning of my birthday. When I awoke, it felt as if I just ran head first into that wall. Sleeplessness and fatigue compounded it all.

That's when I received the best medicine of all – a continuous stream of well wishes, words of affection and encouragement, promises of God that were articulated from the hearts of friends who immediately lifted my spirits. There was even an email packed with encouragement from pastors living in far away Eastern Russia. They had heard the news of my illness and stood in agreement from afar to encourage me through it all.

I also received a FedEx package of letters and “get well” cards from a church on the quaint Island of Molokai. There were social media wishes posted from Central America, Canada, Japan, the Philippines, from saints on the mainland USA and from hundreds others locally in Hawaii. One of my dear brothers in Christ even baked a special birthday cake, and although my condition precluded him from visiting me, he decorated the hallway outside of my hospital room and made sure the cake, filled with encouragement, was delivered to my bedside just in time.

How important is the faith and encouragement of a friend? Note the paralytic in Matthew chapter 9 who was healed not by his own faith, but by the faith of his friends.

> *"Some men brought to him a paralyzed man, lying on a mat. When Jesus saw their faith, he said to the man, 'Take heart, son; your sins are forgiven'"* (Matthew 9:2 NIV).

Isn't it amazing what the faith of friends can do? They were friends who wouldn't stop believing, wouldn't stop praying, who were determined to stop at nothing so that their paralyzed friend could be brought before the feet of Jesus. Because of *THEIR* faith, he was set free.

There are times we'll find ourselves in our own state of "paralysis," when we're unable to move ahead in our own spiritual life. Our marriages may have grown stagnant; we may be in a relationship and we feel like we've been running on a treadmill heading to nowhere; we're trapped in a daily routine with no sense of purpose to fulfill; we're overwhelmed by the weight of financial pressures and personal conflicts that keep us from becoming all that God wants for our lives.

When you find yourself in that state of "paralysis," are there friends who will encourage you forward? Are there friends who love Jesus and love you, in that order, who will stop at nothing to bring you before the feet of Jesus? Perhaps it's time you made a choice to move yourself to a place where you are able to connect with friends who will pour their faith and encouragement upon you when you need it most.

Physically, my energy level remained about four or five (10 being the highest level of energy). But inspirationally, the "injection" of encouragement of faithful friends into my soul sent me ballistic. No one knew exactly what I was going through or how I was feeling, physically or emotionally. No one knew the hopelessness that was brewing in my gut. But that's exactly where I believe this miracle was born. No one needed to know. When we allow encouragement to flow freely from our hearts to that of another, we may never know how it can miraculously bless someone, but it will.

It's the same power that Paul wrote about when we refresh one another's hearts:

> *"Your love has given me great joy and encouragement, because you, brother, have refreshed the hearts of the saints"* (Philemon 1:7 NIV).

And again the writer of Hebrews wrote:

> *"But encourage one another daily, as long as it is called Today, so that none of you may be hardened by sin's deceitfulness"* (Heb. 3:13 NIV).

We may never truly understand what a person may be going through right at that moment when we send off an encouraging word. Send it anyway.

We may never know that a friend may need a reminder of God's hope and love for them. Remind them anyway.

We may never realize how a simple word of inspiration will lift the spirits of another. Inspire them anyway.

The dedicated nursing staff of Queen's Medical Center understood this. As I rested in my room and awaited the arrival of Joy and Jared, feeling a bit lonely, the staff surprised me with an impromptu rendition of "Happy Birthday" accompanied with a slice of Tiramisu!! This was one "injection" brought by the nurses that I would never refuse.

Want to see a miracle? Encourage someone, while it's still today.

Everyone needs encouragement

Encouraging angels - Queen's Medical Center Nurses

Faithful friend celebrating Dad's Birthday

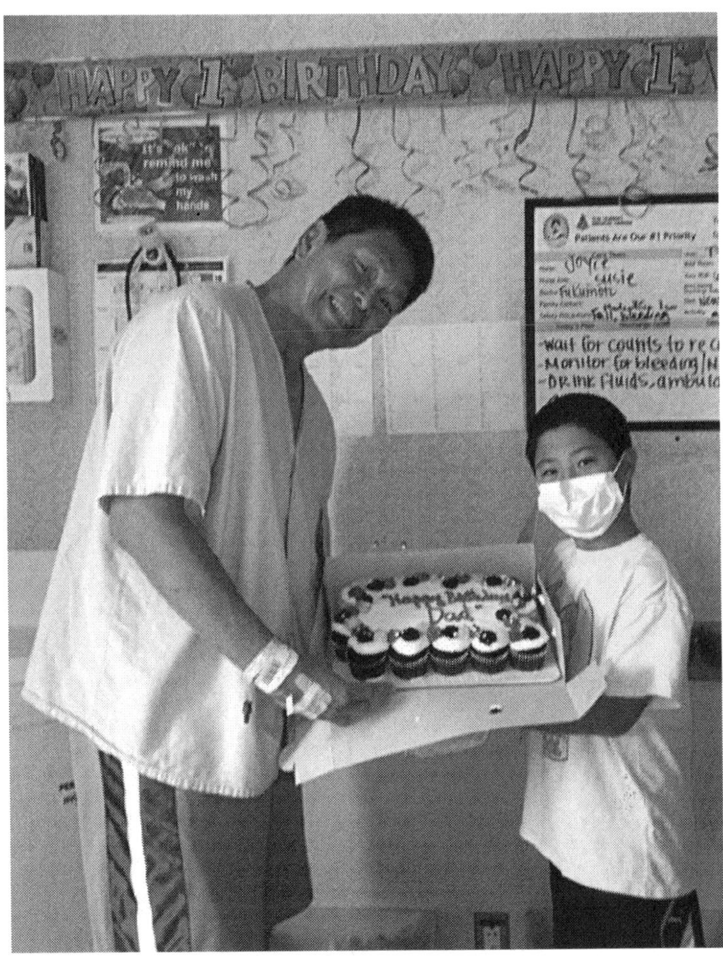
HAPPY 1st BIRTHDAY
HAPPY
remind me
to wash
my
hands
Patients Are Our #1 Priority
Joyce
Susie

Just for Dad!

Hit by the Wall

". . . let us run with endurance the race that is set before us, fixing our eyes on Jesus, the author and perfecter of faith."
(Hebrews 12:1-2 NIV)

What's worse than hitting the wall? When the wall strikes back . . . and there isn't anything you can do about it. The doctors warned me about the day that I'd hit the wall, when every ounce of energy would be drained from my body. No one warned me about the wall hitting back. It struck with a vengeance, intent to lay me out flat. The collision crafted doubt and despair within my spirit, as I considered surrendering to failure, rather than fighting for hope. The wall almost won.

The past few days had been the most unpleasant, nauseating, spirit-deflating days that one could ever imagine . . . that one could never imagine, unless you've been there before. Fatigue struck and it hit hard. In addition, lab results revealed an additional infection had developed with an accompanying fever as life seemed to take another step in the wrong direction. Nights moved beyond miserable. Having a low white cell count only compounded the depressed spirit that began to "toy" with my mind. Open sores and crusted scabs appeared on my torso and I thought of Job and his afflictions:

> *"When I lie down I think, 'How long before I get up?' The night drags on, and I toss and turn until dawn. My body is clothed with worms and scabs, my skin is broken and festering"* (Job 7:4-5).

Another round of antibiotics was prescribed, another IV bag hooked up. Was there ever going to be "light" at the end of the tunnel?

A well-meaning friend tried to encourage me and compared my journey to a marathon race.

"There comes a time in every race when you'll 'hit the wall,'" he said, "but you must push through it if you expect to see the finish line."

I reminded him why I never ran a marathon; I like to see the finish line when I race. This journey was becoming much like a marathon in a multitude of ways. My diagnosis had taken us to the starting blocks. I was assured there would be a finish line – i.e., my discharge – and I'd gain my "freedom" back once again. For the moment, there was still the race to run. Each day became another mile marker to pass and brought me closer to the finish line, but offered yet another challenge. Asking "why" was becoming irrelevant; asking "when" had become nothing but an empty exercise with God.

I'm sure in any marathon, during the course of the race, rookies running for the first time question their own sanity and ask, "Why am I doing this?" or "When is this ever going to end?" Well-wishers, family and friends can cheer from the sidelines, but no one can run that race for that individual. At some point, every runner will hit that infamous and proverbial wall. And when they do, only a determination that arises from within will carry them across the finish line.

What pushed me toward my finish line was when I saw my little guy cry through FaceTime. Jared wasn't able to spend much time with me, due to Joy's cold. In addition, she recently fractured her kneecap and was unable to walk without assistance. We were separated. And that, together with everything else, slammed me. I saw my little guy cry; he missed his dad, he missed his hugs. No one was there to throw the football and baseball with him. Jared missed his dad's cooking.

I saw Brandon doing everything he could to fill in for me. He was big brother to Jared and a loving son to Joy. He surprised her with flowers and balloons, as well as lunch to cheer her up. And that fueled my fire. I may have hit the wall, but I was still alive. I was still in the race; I wasn't giving up. And so I *willed* myself to cross that finish line with a determination that I could only draw from within my soul.

Running life's marathon is no different. Along the route, we'll be confronted and tested beyond our expectancy or presented with unforeseen challenges. In other words, we'll hit a "wall" that stands in the face of our family or finances, or it will strike our health when we least expect it. But despite its attempts to derail us from our journey, it will take a determination that can only arise from deep within our soul to press us to finish the race well – a determination forged from that which we value more than ourselves.

> "*... let us run with perseverance the race marked out for us . . .*" (Hebrews12:1NIV).

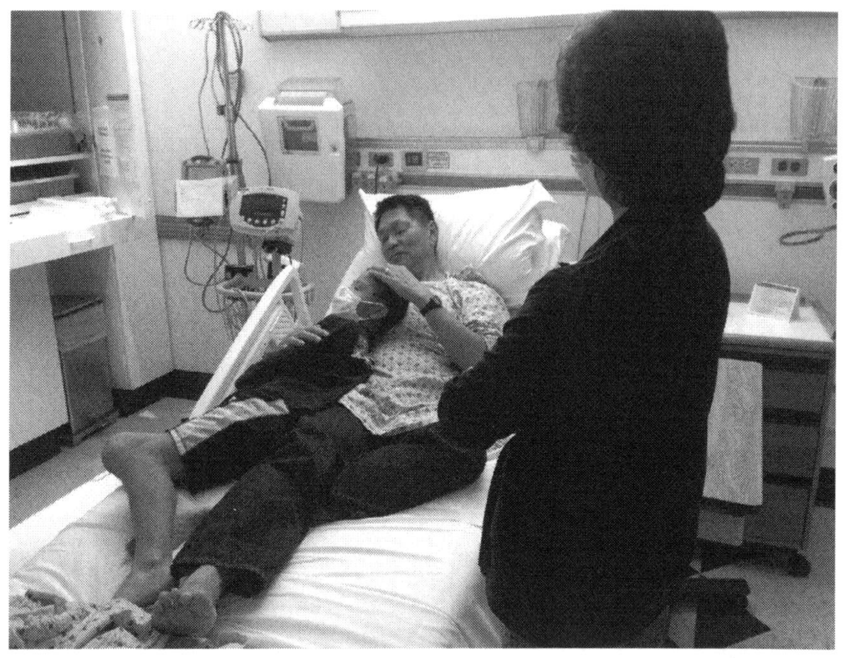

Not ready to go home; just one more hug, please.

Gifts Strangely Wrapped

"If God is for us, who can be against us?
He who did not spare his own Son,
but gave Him up for us all – how will He not also,
along with Him, graciously give us all things?"
(Romans 8:31-32 NIV)

Brandon and Jared put up the Christmas tree in the Ahu household. It was a little later than to be expected, but what else was different with the Ahus these days? I wanted so badly to have been there, if for no other reason than to make sure these two "young men" knew there was a difference between the top and bottom of an artificial tree set. (I'm proud of their success; worried for their wives).

But it was Jared's apparent observation that caught my attention.

"Mom," he asked, "now that the tree is up, where are all the gifts that I normally see under it?" (Note: Before breaking out the tissues, know that his aunties and uncles had it all covered). His question challenged me on my road to recovery.

Last night was another "typical" night that summoned my energy reserves to battle a relentless fever, continuous chills and headaches that robbed me of another night's sleep. Added to my misery were the periodic interruptions to take my vitals, blood samples, midnight medications, etc. It exhausted my energy reserves, but it was expected.

What I didn't expect was the lack of a definitive timeline to my release date. My "escape" from the hospital depended upon my body's ability to reproduce a sustainable source of good, healthy white cells. Those cells would strengthen my immunity against the viruses and bacteria that exist everywhere in this world. And there was nothing I could do, except wait and let nature – spelled G-O-D – take its course. In other words, there was no "normal" pattern that I could hang my hopes upon. Was I discouraged? Absolutely and increasingly as time ticked by!

The morning's lab report indicated an even lower white cells count than the day before, and to add insult to injury, my platelet count had also plummeted. Without sufficient platelets, traces of blood appeared in my nasal discharge and triggered the cycle of questions and doubts once again.

"Was this normal?"

"Was it simply to be expected?"

"Was there a pattern of recovery that one could expect, similar to the recovering cycle from a common cold or the mending of broken bones?"

There is no greater destroyer of hope than the unknown. It's what fills the future for many of us. And that was exactly the spirit of Jared's question around the Christmas tree. Like Jared, we all have expectations, whether they're listed as goals, crafted as letters to "Santa," shouted out and demanded, or allowed to silently simmer in our spirits as a series of entitlements. And unless they are satisfied, unless our anticipated conditions have been met, then life just isn't good enough, and there must be something wrong with God.

Unfulfilled expectations can give us universal license to say whatever we want against God whenever we want, especially when the pain and suffering compound itself. Unforeseen complications raise their ugly heads around every corner. We shrink back into despair, resigned to presume that God must not hear us. Therefore, why ask and why pray, as we allow hope to fade away.

This is where my little guy "saved my life," yet again. His question prompted me to look beyond the "natural," oftentimes blurred by my limited human comprehension. If we want to see the "supernatural" gifts God strangely wrapped for us to discover, we need eyes to see what God is seeing. When we look with the limitations of our human mindset, we pre-determine our own destinies and set our own hearts on expectations that we have no control over. This default isn't limited to uncharted cancer treatment plans, but we also apply it to life in general, such as when we question whether "Santa" will receive our letters addressed to the North Pole, or whether God does indeed hear prayers we've repeatedly raised toward heaven.

When we try to make sense of the insensible, we set ourselves up for disappointment, doubt, depression and defeat. In our confusion, we naturally search for and hinge our hopes on what we believe will create a sense of normalcy that we expect to function like a gyroscope used to settle a ship in a stormy seas. In the stormy seas of life's confusing mess, we long for our circumstances to return to a state of normalcy and balance our unsettled spirit.

"Normalcy" can't be dependent on what *we* expect, whether it's an expected treatment plan, release date or even God's intervention to heal according to our terms and on our conditions. Normalcy must be based on one thing, that which never changes – the promises of God. Just as Moses reassured Joshua, God's Word reassures us today

> *"The Lord himself goes before you and will be with you; He will never leave you nor forsake you. Do not be afraid; do not be discouraged"* (Deuteronomy 31:8 NIV).

Catch that? Our Lord never leaves us, nor will He ever allow us on this journey alone. So, in the confusion and mess of life, there is only one thing that we can be certain of: "God is with us AND God is for us."

I asked the doctor, "Is what I'm experiencing 'normal?' I can handle the pain (that was a lie), I can handle the fever (another lie), if only I knew this was part of a normal overall progression of my treatment."

My doctor, a man of few words, replied, "Yes."

I found it interesting that once I was assured of what was "normal," it gave me new eyes to see what I'd been missing.

My attention shifted from the fevers, chills, nausea and all-around discomfort, from what I didn't know to what I now did know. Based upon what I knew, any unanswered prayer or the gifts that weren't under the tree became irrelevant. Instead, I began to see, through new eyes, the "gifts" strangely wrapped, that I had already received:

- I was diagnosed and began treatment just in time
- Two weeks of treatment were history, never to be repeated again
- Intensive rounds of chemotherapy were completed
- No more IV needles protruding from my arm

- My specialists were two of the best
- Fluctuating blood counts were normal
- Friends who prayed, loved and supported my family and me
- My family
- God who will never give up on me

The list went on.

In all honesty, there was a time when I thought I'd never be able to say Christmas would be "merry." After all that had transpired – fevers that spiked through the night, ice packs that covered me to stabilize my temperature, the flood of antibiotics squeezed through my veins (I don't think even the devil can survive in me anymore), nausea and endless reactions to chemotherapy – I thought Christmas morning would be anything but "merry." Living on intermittent intervals sleep of no more than an hour and feeling constantly yucky gave me no incentive to be merry.

Here's what I've learned along the way: God remains faithful! Life is unfair, but God is faithful. Cancer is unjust, but God will never give up on me, nor will He forsake me. The process of recovery sucks! But my God provides a peace that transcends all understanding, and He guards my heart and mind.

So guess what God saved for my Christmas morning:

- I woke up to the most beautiful sunrise and with the most energy I've felt in a long time; I felt I could have checked out!

- Fever was my body's way of saying it was ready to fight back against what was trying to defeat me
- Brandon "snuck in" wun tun mein[8] for lunch – and I practically swallowed the whole meal with one bite!
- I still had hair on my head!
- I was honored to watch our church's Christmas Eve service with Joy via FaceTime. Our volunteers seemed more committed to Christ than ever;
- Brandon knocked his first-ever Christmas message "out of the park" (okay, I'm biased, but this experience has launched his leadership into the next level of his gifting).

God is so faithful that He saved my best gift for last:

- On Christmas, it was the first night since my admission that I was able to sleep practically through the night. Except for one medicine change out, it turned out to be one of the most restful nights I had yet!

GOD IS FAITHFUL! And yes, it was a Merry Christmas after all! All I wanted for this Christmas . . . not a thing. I already had all that I needed.

---

[8] A Chinese dish made of noodles and broth, with pork-filled dumplings and vegetables.

"Who shall separate us from the love of Christ? Shall trouble or hardship or persecution or famine or nakedness or danger or sword? As it is written: 'For your sake we face death all day long; we are considered as sheep to be slaughtered.' No, in all these things we are more than conquerors through Him who loved us. For I am convinced that neither death nor life, neither angels nor demons, neither the present nor the future, nor any powers, neither height nor depth, nor anything else in all creation, will be able to separate us from the love of God that is in Christ Jesus our Lord" (Rom. 8:35-39 NIV).

Don't know how Dad it by himself!

Hanging that special one for Dad

Ruthless Trust

"Though He slay me, yet I will hope in Him."
(Job 13:15 NIV)

I had spent 21 days in the hospital, and counting. By all other standards governing the discipline of human behavior, it normally takes 21 days to turn a person's actions into a habit. Now, don't misunderstand, but although I was cared for in a compassionate and professionally run medical facility, pampered by some of the best nursing staff and doctors, I didn't intend to turn my ordeal into a habit. I couldn't wait to go home.

Yet, there was a purpose in me being there – for every blood sample drawn at the crack of dawn, for each injected round of chemo through my veins, for the multiple bags of antibiotics, for the daily transfusions of blood and platelets into my system, for the pills and medications I was compelled to take. God's purpose rested beyond simply the medical necessities.

God is a God of order, not chaos. He's a God of choice and not chance. He is a God who knows the plans established for us, not for our calamity, but plans to prosper us, to give us a future and a hope (Jeremiah 29:11). So, in the midst of the 21 straight days of chaos, I knew that there was a rare gem God wanted me to mine from the depths of this experience. If I missed it, I would be poorer because of it.

At this juncture, I pressed into the Father to see what His purpose was for me. What spiritual discipline was He attempting to form into a "habit" throughout my journey? His response: to develop within me the passion to trust Him regardless of the circumstances or conditions, regardless of the unanswered questions or the unknowns.

It's what author Brennan Manning described in his book

"*Ruthless Trust: The Ragamuffin's Path to God*" (Harper Collins, 2000). He defines "Ruthless Trust" as the "walk on water" kind of trust. It's a trust like Abraham's that led him to the mountaintop and obediently place his only son, Isaac, on the sacrificial altar, without question and without doubts, trusting that God had a greater plan at hand. It's the kind of trust that kept Jesus walking toward His crucifixion and carrying His cross, regardless how heavy the burden became, or how painful the suffering.

In his book, Manning posed the defining question that confronts every one of us at the intersection of suffering: "Can God be trusted?" He engages the reader in a conversation that develops the concept of trust beyond a superficial intellectual assent to a deeper experience of joy in *passionately* trusting God.

> *"The way of trust is a movement into obscurity, into the undefined, into ambiguity, not into some predetermined, clearly delineated plan for the future. The next step discloses itself only out of a discernment of God acting in the desert of the present moment. The reality of naked trust is the life of the pilgrim who leaves what is nailed down, obvious, and secure, and walks into the unknown without any rational explanation to justify the decision or guarantee the future. Why? Because God has signaled the movement and offered it his presence and his promise."*

For the last 21 days, I became the pilgrim Manning described who was forced to leave the comfort and convenience and sent into the unknown. My pilgrimage launched me into a land beyond the obvious where there was no one that I could trust more than my God. He orchestrated it all for me to capture the deeper essence of this experience. He had even removed the security of my own family from me in order to help me to develop not simply a superficial assent of Him, but to have a passion for His trust and love for me.

During one of my worst reactions to my chemo treatment, when I needed my family the most, why else was no one able to be there for me? Joy developed a fever, and both Brandon and Jared contracted coughs that prohibited them from visiting my hospital room. And if that weren't enough, why else was I stricken with Chicken Pox, (at my age), an infectious disease that kept me in isolation. I wasn't permitted to leave my room and no one was allowed in.

It was in my loneliest moment that I discovered that God was "*acting in the desert of the present*" and offered in it His presence and His promise. Why was I led into this season of suffering? It was because He wanted to develop within me a deep and passionate love and trust for my truest friend, my Father. Listen to how Manning describes this level of trust:

> *"The splendor of a human heart that trusts it is loved unconditionally gives God more pleasure than Westminster Cathedral, the Sistine Chapel, Beethoven's 'Ninth Symphony', Van Gogh's 'Sunflowers,' the sight of 10,000 butterflies in flight, or the scent of a million orchids in bloom. Trust is our gift back to God, and he finds it so enchanting that Jesus died for love of it."*

God affirmed this gift on an evening when all was quiet on the floor and I experienced a divine appointment with a nurse who had visited me in the dark of the night. It was a conversation I will never forget.

"I checked your files; you're a pastor right?" she asked.

"Yes," I replied, not wanting to prolong the conversation. I was exhausted and wanted to sleep.

"What did you do before that?" she continued to press.

"I was a judge," I answered. It was late; I was nauseous and de-energized. I didn't have any desire to share more than what I just said and hoped she wouldn't ask me to share my "judge turned pastor" testimony.

"So, you're a big-shot leader? I've had other patients who were big leaders. You know what your problem is?" She now sounded like my *sensei*, my teacher, trying to impress her student with a point to take home.

"What's my problem?" I sheepishly submitted.

She continued, "You're no longer in control. As a pastor, I bet you thought you'd be visiting patients in the hospital, rather than being one."

"Touché," I responded. "What's your point?"

And to that, she said what I believe captured the full essence of my being in the hospital on this unwelcomed journey.

"When you wake up tomorrow morning, you need to learn how to trust the doctors, trust the nurses and trust God. Can I pray for you?"

As she extended her hands to me, feeling like I was just schooled by an angel of the Lord, I reached out to take ahold of hers. She prayed, left my room, and I never saw that nurse again. My angel of God visited me that night and my life has not been the same.

"Though He slay me, yet I will hope in him" (Job 13:15).

No Greater Love

"Greater love has no one than this:
to lay down one's life for one's friend."
(John15:13)

My fever persisted and tenaciously tested my will as the battle continued to rage on. Overnight, nurses packed ice bags on my head and chest and under my neck and arms, and trying to lower my body temperature to medically acceptable levels. Chills caused my body to shake uncontrollably. I ached in every joint. The day wasn't looking good. The only saving grace: Joy's planned visit after she attended church.

The morning seemed to only get longer as I counted the minutes before her arrival. But my fever wasn't cooperating. While I waited, my feverish sweat soaked my bed sheets and clothes that required multiple changes. I didn't feel like seeing anyone except Joy. Little did I expect what was about to happen once she arrived.

It was lunchtime and I didn't have an appetite for hospital food. To increase my caloric intake that would aid in my recovery, the doctors had previously given Joy permission to order food from any outside restaurants for my meals. When she arrived, I asked if she could order take-out from a nearby fast food restaurant.

On any other day, Joy would have graciously complied. Today, she seemed a bit anxious and hesitant, but she eventually left and returned with my meal. While she was gone, my fever spiked again. I halfheartedly ate a few bites from the lunch she bought. She then insisted that I walk with her down the hall.

"Didn't she understand? I wasn't feeling well," I thought. She called the nurse's station and asked for another round of medication and maintained once more that we take a walk. I could barely stand. With her help, I prepared myself and held on to the rolling IV tower as a balance. Steadying myself against the hallway wall, I slowly made my way down the long length of the corridor that seemed much longer than the day before. I was bundled in a white hooded sweater, still shivering from chills and fever. The walk seemed like an eternity. Why did Joy all of a sudden become my drill sergeant? When we arrived at a window opening down the hall, it all became clear.

Gathered on the rooftop of an adjacent parking structure were more than 100 well-wishers holding banners and balloons, signs and streamers and pom-poms poised to explode into an exuberant cheer . . . for me. Their excitement was contagious and quickly destroyed any feeling of hopelessness and despair that was brewing within me. But there was one obstacle: the hospital's window tint was too dark for anyone from the outside of the hospital to see in. Joy and I could see them, but the crowd wasn't able to see us.

Using her smartphone, Joy quickly called the masterminds of this surprise, Kea and Alex, and she described where we were standing. They amplified her voice through speakerphones to the crowd, who erupted in cheer when they heard we were at the window looking out at them. The intensity of their cheering penetrated into the surrounding valley and into the hallway where we stood. To give them a better visual of us, I slipped out of my white sweater and pressed it against the windowpanes, using a wiping motion for them to see. It worked. Every movement of my sweater across the tinted glass triggered another round of cheers; confetti and streamers burst into the air, laughter, cries of joy overflowed from their hearts . . . and overwhelmed ours.

These people weren't just members of a church. They were our friends who were willing to give up their Sunday afternoon, to sacrifice a moment of their life to express how much they loved us. They were willing to set love before anything that mattered, at that moment, for that time. Joy explained later how the entire escapade was planned in just a few hours at church that morning. It was why she insisted that I walked down the hallway, regardless of how I felt.

Words fail to describe how such love from our friends gave me life that day. It was more than any medication could have done for my fever, more than any medical professional could have advised. Our friends were willing to lay down their lives for us, and in doing so, it gave me a renewed will to continue to fight the good fight. It was exactly the medicine that I needed.

- ☐ Is there someone who could use a word of encouragement from you today?

- ☐ Is there someone who could benefit from the sacrifice of your time, shared word of hope, a visit or a moment to lift their spirits?

Greater love has no one than this: to lay one's life down for one's friend (John 15:13 NIV). Dare to be a friend today.

Not just friends; we're family!

“Greater love has no one than this: to lay down one’s life for one’s friend (John 15:13).”

Be Still

"Be still and know that I am God."
(Psalm 46:10 NIV)

What were you doing when the clock struck the delineating divide between 2012 and 2013? Or, perhaps the question should be, "What were you thinking?" Were your thoughts focused on the past or about the future, or both?

Needless to say, being confined to a hospital room on New Year's Eve was never part of my 20-year life plan. While others celebrated the end of their year with parties and indulged in sashimi, sushi, steak, shrimp tempura, festivities and entertainment, my body decided to put on its own "fireworks" exhibition. It was as if I was caught in the crossfire of chemotherapy and antibiotics that aimed at every cell in sight to wipe out the old, in order to welcome the production of new cells. Its consequences were nothing to celebrate, however. Fever struck once more. So, as pyrotechnics filled the air in every community across the islands, at the stroke of midnight my body unleashed a fireworks display of its own as every cell within me seemed to be on fire. I was completely soaked in sweat from head to toe . . . again.

Fever was having its way in me. My body temperature spiked to over 102 degrees. Chills thrust me into uncontrollable convulsive shivers that literally rocked my bed so violently as if it was a scene from the classic thriller, *"The Exorcist."* I just wanted the world to go away. The nurses changed my bedding and clothes, once . . . then again . . . and again a few hours later. The new morning of a new year was anything but "new" for me. I experienced the same sleepless night lying in the same discomfort on drenched and saturated sheets. This persisted through the remaining hours of the evening as the door swung open into 2013.

I was tired . . . tired of hospital food; tired of the scent and smell of hospital soap and cleansing solutions; tired of the mounds of fallen hair that blanketed my sheets and clogged the shower drain. I was hesitant to towel-dry my head after a shower, disgusted at the sight of hair I'd find matted in the towel. Baldness was well on its way. I was tired of the loneliness at night, of not being able to cuddle with my son or to lie next to my wife, to feel her arms around me.

As Joy prepared to leave after spending the day, she knew something wasn't right in my spirit.

"What's wrong?" she asked.

"I'm just tired of all of this," I frustratingly replied, as my spirit entered the "valley of despair" once again. I sequentially recalled everything we had done, the sacrifices we made, what we had given our lives for, all "in the name of Jesus," and yet, I was still stricken with this disease. It wasn't fair and I demanded to know why.

Sensing my defeated spirit, and trying to empathize with me, Joy reasoned, "Perhaps it's so that you will be able to better understand the suffering of other people; so as a pastor, you will know exactly what they're going through."

"I don't buy that," I retorted. I know she meant well, but I was tired. I didn't want to hear anyone try to placate me with some "spiritual" lesson.

"If that's true," I argued back, looking to lawyerly prove my point, "then every bed next to me should be filled with other pastors so they, too, can understand what it means to suffer." I quickly snapped back with the names of a few pastors that in my frustration I thought should be suffering more than me right now. "Why me? What was I being recruited for this task?" I thought.

To this, Joy, in true merciful fashion, kindly responded, "Then maybe the Lord has such faith in us to trust us to walk the path of suffering that He walked, knowing that we won't give up."

Have you ever felt like God just knocked you clear across the forehead with a "holy 2 x 4" piece of wood and said, "Wake up!!" That's exactly what the Holy Spirit did with the words Joy shared. Maybe this whole ordeal wasn't about trying to understand "why" or trying to make sense of it all. Perhaps the struggle wasn't supposed to be a struggle after all, but a celebration of the Lord's trust in me. He saw more faith in me than I saw in myself. He trusted me to have the same faith that He had when He walked the road of suffering all the way to Calvary. Perhaps He knew we could be trusted to suffer, so that we would also share in His glory.

> *"The Spirit himself testifies with our spirit that we are God's children. Now if we are children, then we are heirs—heirs of God and co-heirs with Christ, if indeed we share in his sufferings in order that we may also share in his glory"* (Romans 8:16-17 NIV).

But I had to choose to not give up. There was no other option, regardless how much more was thrown at me. Quitting could not be in my vocabulary.

Therein lurked the challenge of applying such an attitudinal perspective to the realities of what I was assigned to endure. There really was nothing I could do to incite, invigorate or influence my body to get better. As an athlete who has trained for championship competition in the past, I knew how to set a goal for myself, to discipline my body to train and sacrifice in order to get the results I desired. As a leader, I've learned to do the same. The key to my recovery, however, rested upon the capacity of my bone marrow to generate healthy, fresh white and red blood cells and platelets. My fevers were an indication that that process had begun, but it was a process that would take time – and only God knew how long. There was nothing I could do about it.

So, I was left to be still and know that He is God. As one of the nurses reminded me, "Your responsibility is to just breathe; let God and the staff take care of the rest." It brought new meaning to the verses I recited each night as I mediated myself to sleep:

> *"Trust in the Lord with all your heart and lean not on your understanding; in all your ways acknowledge Him, and He will make your paths straight"* (Proverbs 3:5-6 NIV).
>
> *"But those who hope (wait, trust) in The Lord will renew their strength. They will soar on wings like eagles; they will run and not grow weary, they will walk and not faint"* (Isa. 40:31 NIV).
>
> *"Do not be anxious about anything, but in everything, by prayer and petition, with thanksgiving, present your requests to God. And the peace of God, which transcends all understanding, will guard*

> *your hearts and your minds in Christ Jesus"* (Philip. 4:6-7 NIV).

I was heading into the toughest stretch of this journey. The end seemed so close, yet with all that my body was expected to tolerate and endure in the days ahead, the finish line seemed so far away. My only hope: be still and rest in His promise, that regardless of the burden, He would be there to carry me to the other side.

One of the many "Get Well" cards that I received contained a poem that spoke to my heart and encouraged me for the journey.

"Footprints"

One night I had a dream.
I dreamed I was walking along the beach with the Lord,
And across the sky flashed scenes from my life.
For each scene I noticed two sets of footprints in the sand;
One belonged to me, and the other to the Lord.
When the last scene of my life flashed before us,
I looked back at the footprints in the sand.
I noticed that many times along the path of my life,
There was only one set of footprints.
I also noticed that it happened at the very lowest
And saddest times in my life.
This really bothered me, and I questioned the Lord about it.
"Lord, you said that once I decided to follow you,
You would walk with me all the way;
But I have noticed that during the most troublesome times in my life, there is only one set of footprints.

I don't understand why in times when I needed you the most, you should leave me."

The Lord replied, "My precious, precious child.
I love you, and I would never, never leave you
During your times of trial and suffering.
When you saw only one set of footprints,
It was then that I carried you."
(Anonymous)

My Shepherd, My Friend

"The Lord is my shepherd, I shall not want."
(Psalm 23:1 NASB)

Thirty days had passed since registering in this "hotel." Although there were the "perks" of a hotel – changed bedding and "room service" – it was a far cry from being a vacation resort. Obviously, there were no pools, fancy ballrooms or five-star fine dining. The view – rooftops and parking garages. It wouldn't be surprising to learn that every registered "guest" would have rather been somewhere else than here. But with all that this place was not, it became the perfect greenhouse for the seeds of God's Word to germinate and take root in me. The realities of God's truths reached into the depths of my heart like never before.

Being here, as senseless as it may have initially seemed, served as an incubator where I experienced the fruits of God's promises that had once been planted in me, and where the power of His Word was nurtured by prayers that were offered in the midst of tears, loneliness and desperation. It was here that I experienced the hope and resurrection power that are ours to inherit.

> *"I pray that the eyes of your heart may be enlightened in order that you may know the hope to which he has called you, the riches of his glorious inheritance in his holy people, and his incomparably great power for us who believe. That power is the same as the mighty strength he exerted when he raised Christ from the dead and seated him at his right hand in the heavenly realms"* (Ephesians 1:18-19 NIV).

Here where the sick and afflicted resided, God's Word breathed life into a dry and parched soul, and sowed seeds of hope while I laid in the dark days of my suffering. In the loneliness of the night, Jesus became simply my Shepherd and my Friend for both my family and me.

Having experienced the valley, I can say with absolute certainty that I now know the Shepherd. The journey was not an easy one to travel; obviously not for me, but neither for the rest of our family. In an instant, Joy became my primary caregiver and head of our household. More importantly, she became the only pillar of strength for a weeping child who tried to make sense of it all. How does a 10-year-old boy – or for that matter, even a grown son at 31 years old – come to grips with the reality of potentially losing his dad? Would their children ever have a grandfather to spoil them? Would this be their last celebration of their dad's birthday, Christmas and New Year's?

I don't believe anyone can fully comprehend the impact of imminent death, unless and until the Almighty "permits" him or her to come face to face with its ugly sting. It's one thing to recite Scriptures about hope and sing and preach about God's promises. However, when you've been asked to live it, when you've been positioned to stand at the threshold of death's doorway and stare at its dark shadows cast in the valley, death and dying takes on an entirely different perspective. We stood exactly at that place, but there were no fears in any of us. We understood death, but we chose to live. When our emotions overwhelmed us, our God remained faithful; His rod and His staff lovingly and graciously embraced us.

> *"Even though I walk through the valley of the shadow of death, I fear no evil, for You are with me; Your rod and Your staff, they comfort me"* (Ps. 23:4 NIV).

Through it all, regardless how many more days I needed to remain as a "registered guest," what may have been thrown our way or attempted to divide our family, we chose to stand on one truth:

"The Lord, He is our Shepherd, and we shall not want. He will provide, just as He has provided, everything that we'll ever need."

Turn the Page

"For just as we share abundantly in the sufferings of Christ,
so also our comfort abounds through Christ."
(2 Corinthians 1:5 NIV)

IT WAS TIME!! My blood count finally reached acceptable levels. The doctors cleared me and it was finally time to go home! I felt like shouting, "Hallelujah; give praises to the King!" I always believed I would be released one day; it was just a matter of time. But to actually hear the doctor say, "You can go home today," opened a floodgate of emotions and just about brought me to my knees.

I was "chauffeured" out of the hospital and for the first time in 30 days, I breathed my first breath of fresh air, felt my first rays of sunshine, and smelled the sweet scent of blossoming flowers. Jared had no idea I was being released. We surprised him and picked him up from school.

One of the great joys in the world is seeing the expression of a son when he meets his dad after a long absence. We shared a hug that can only be measured by the degree of how much he missed his dad. But now, he got to rejoice in the renewal of hope. Certain events in life simply cannot be described adequately in words, and the joyful embrace of a child who longed for his dad is definitely one of them. I can only imagine the embrace we will share with our Heavenly Father when we finally get to stand in His presence!

Today, I consider my life richer because of the pages God added to the unfinished story of my life. On each page, He used the pain and suffering to tell a story of His faithfulness as He walked with me though my ordeal. I never imagined these chapters would be mine, but the script was written nonetheless. In the sovereignty of God's storyline, He challenged me to press through the realities of His suffering, to walk in total dependence and trust, and to grasp onto the power of prayer. He led me to find hope in His grace in my times of weakness.

Because He trusted me to "share abundantly in the sufferings of Christ," I trusted Him. God dictated and I obeyed. Each day I positioned myself to stand at the threshold of a new chapter. They weren't easy chapters to write, but I am forever grateful that God had enough faith to entrust me with a season of suffering, so that He could fill the blank pages of my life with a testimony of trust.

In the beginning, God created the heavens and the earth, and all that was in it . . . and "saw that it was good." Being home from the hospital, I couldn't agree more that what God saw in the beginning was good. There hasn't been a morning that has gone by where I don't find myself staring in awe at the glowing hues of purple and pink of the morning's sunrise, feeling the fresh, cool mountain breeze brush across my face, or hearing the sweet song of birds that welcome in their new day. With each moment, I continually thank the Lord for giving me breath to enjoy the goodness of His creation.

With each new day, I've gained more strength. If you've never walked down this road before, it would be hard to imagine the muscle strength you lose and the challenge to accomplish even the simplest task. But every day seemed to renew my strength. I started to cook again, which proved to be especially therapeutic for me: chicken, squash and tofu soup; baked salmon with dill and garlic sauce; and a nice thick juicy steak with grilled onions, baked potato smothered with sour cream!

Through this journey, it's as if God granted me a new beginning to appreciate the simple things He's already created, to fall in love with Him all over again. 2 Corinthians 5:17 reminds us that *"if anyone is in Christ, the new creation has come: The old has gone, the new is here!"* I can shout "Amen" to that! Through blood transfusions, I'm filled – literally – with new blood and new platelets. The chemo has destroyed just about every cell in my body, only to see new and healthy cells regenerate to replace the old. I've lost hair strands by the hundreds, if not thousands, only to have new strands stand in place of the old. Even my skin experienced a metamorphosis from the old into the new, peeling and shedding old skin cells and resurrected new skin in its place. The old has passed, the new is here!

Every morning, I'm greeted with a fresh start. I can't wait to embrace it! Whatever course I am required to take, I know that my Redeemer lives and in this season of new beginnings I will *"sing to The Lord a new song, for He has done marvelous things"* (Psalm 98:1 NIV). I shall walk in confidence, knowing that *"the Lord is my light and salvation, whom shall I fear . . . whom shall I be afraid? . . . I will see the goodness of The Lord in the land of the living*" (Psalm 27:1, 13 NIV).

Here's what I wrote in my journal to memorialize that special day:

> *Now, it's time to turn the page, to move obediently into what The Lord has written for me next. I don't know what, I don't know where, I certainly won't question why, but I know that God has an assignment for me to apply all that I've been through. I don't know what it is that HE wants for me, but this I do know – that in His time He will reveal it, and when He does, I know it will be for His Kingdom, it will be for His honor and glory. I just need to*

be obedient and trust Him, fully, completely and faithfully. It will be within this next chapter that He will reveal yet another miracle.

My heart is overwhelmed with gratefulness for the prayers of the saints that poured in daily from around the world. Without each prayer, I would not be home today. Ready? Here we go, turn the page. See you in the next chapter.

Lord, may I never lose the thrill of hugging my wife and my kids, of feeling our spirits fuse as one. May I never lose the excited anticipation of being reunited with my friends and the love of the saints and the gratefulness of their prayers. Thank You for allowing me to sweep ever so close to death so that I could discover and appreciate life as You created it to be, in the beginning.

Free at last!!

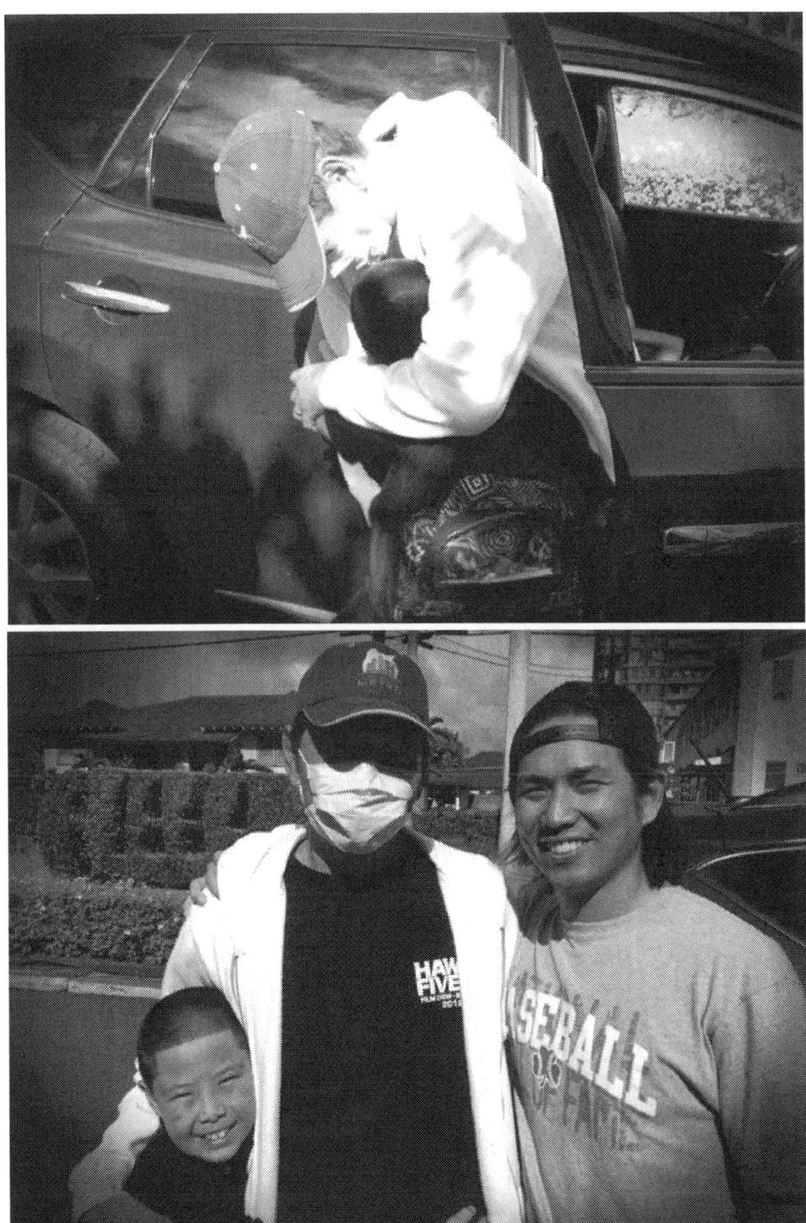

When the love of a father is embraced by his sons.

The Price of Obedience

"And so after waiting patiently,
Abraham received what was promised."
(Hebrews 6:15 NIV)

There are moments in the Bible that, upon first reading, begs you to do a double take and ask, "Did God really mean what He just said?"

Abraham's life was filled with moments like these. In Genesis 15, for example, immediately following God's promise that Abraham's descendants would fill the earth as the stars fill the heavens and would possess the Promised Land, God slapped Abraham with the "right hand of reality":

> *"Then the Lord said to him, 'Know for certain that* **for four hundred years** *your descendants will be strangers in a country not their own and that they will be enslaved and mistreated there. But I will punish the nation they serve as slaves, and afterward they will come out with great possessions'"* (Genesis 15:13-14 NIV).

Did you catch that? To those who would inherit the promise, they first needed to suffer, not just for a year, two years, or 20, but for 400 years! For what seemed like an eternity, Abraham's children, grandchildren and great grandchildren, fell into an extended season of suffering, hardship and distress that were wrapped and packaged in the bondage of slavery. And only *after* their suffering would the promise be fulfilled. In faith, Abraham never questioned and he never doubted the promises of God.

That's what I find so intriguing about this elderly, aging man of faith. Regardless of what others might have considered to be the ridiculousness of God, Abraham saw it as the righteousness of His Master. He never disbelieved. He simply obeyed.

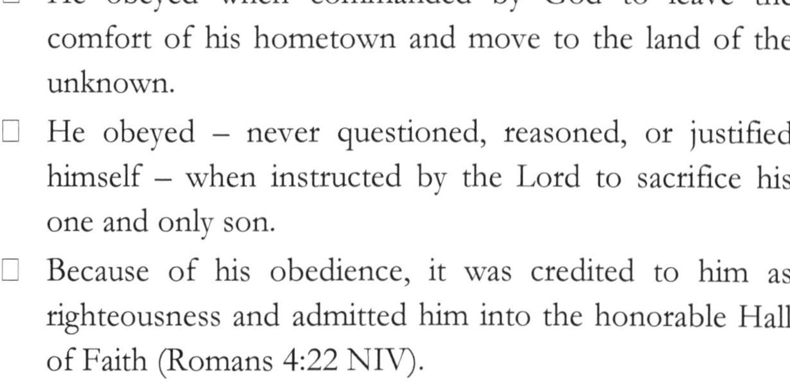

- He obeyed when commanded by God to leave the comfort of his hometown and move to the land of the unknown.
- He obeyed – never questioned, reasoned, or justified himself – when instructed by the Lord to sacrifice his one and only son.
- Because of his obedience, it was credited to him as righteousness and admitted him into the honorable Hall of Faith (Romans 4:22 NIV).

My own journey landed me on the battlefield against leukemia and if it taught me anything, I now understand more completely the price that obedience demands. God will never hide His promises that are filled with His blessings. But I wonder how many blessings we fail to realize when we refuse to pay the price of obedience, i.e., to incur its cost through our suffering, regardless of the consequences.

Yesterday was my second follow up with my doctor since being released from the hospital. My journey continued to expose me to the truth of God's Word. It had been just 10 days since I gained freedom that allowed me to enjoy the sunset walks with my wife and strengthened my physical and emotional well-being. Our family enjoyed 10 days of basking in the warmth of our family hugs. But I learned how life has a habit of interrupting all good things.

After undergoing a second bone marrow biopsy (ouch!), the doctor ordered another round of hospitalization and chemo treatments. Although the leukemia was more than likely in remission, more treatments were necessary to clear me completely of the disease. So, I returned to "the desert" once more. In total, my treatment required me to be hospitalized for 59 days. Any separation from my family was one day too long. But, if I intended to walk into His Promise and receive the blessing of being completely free of every destructive leukemic cell, then I could not doubt or question the doctor's prognosis and plan. I needed to be willing to pay the price of obedience – to be willing to suffer for the sake of the promise.

This is no different from whatever God may ask of us. His plans are always tied to a promise for our families, for our marriages, for our lives. But in order to realize His precious promises, the price of obedience must be paid. We must possess a willingness to suffer for the sake of the promise, regardless of the degree of difficulty.

Just as Jesus paid the price on the cross in order to realize the promise of the resurrection, so, too, must we be willing to stand ready to respond, "Father, not my will, but may Thy will be done." And when that price is paid, His Word assures us that, "Though the sorrow may last for the night, His joy comes in the morning" (Psalm 30:5 NIV).

Defeating Depression

"The weapons we fight with are not the weapons of the world. On the contrary, they have divine power to demolish strongholds . . . and we take captive every thought to make it obedient to Christ."
(2 Corinthians 10:4-5 NIV)

"Depression" can be summed up in a dirty five-letter word: it's "nasty, cruel and it kills." Its desire is to drain every bit of hope and suck the spirit of joy from a person's soul. How do I know? It tried to take me down.

Spending a total of 59 days in the hospital cost me more than dollars and cents. I had become "institutionalized." I had grown dependent on the availability of a nursing staff, that at the press of a button trained medical personnel would answer and address whatever was needed in order to return me to a state of comfort. Whether it was a headache or to alleviate the nausea, there was always a team of doctors, nurses, aides standing by ready to respond.

Being at home, however, left me feeling alone and vulnerable. What if I needed immediate attention to address a life-threatening condition? What if that slight pain in my chest was the beginnings of a heart attack? What if I suddenly couldn't lift my arms? Without the immediate availability of any medical staff, "Google" became my "advisory board." I became my own doctor, nurse, aide, all rolled into one – bad mistake. Every symptom I "researched" on the Internet listed hundreds of side effects, precautions and additional warning signs and painted the worst-case scenario that only heightened my anxiety levels. My spirits spiraled downward. Although I was home and hospital-free, and this was supposed to be the best time of my life, my anxiety increased by the day. Hopelessness took residence in my heart once again and I couldn't regain control.

Depression stepped in and interrupted my sleep patterns. Insomnia haunted me, as I found myself diving deeper and deeper into irrational and senseless thoughts that kept me awake all night. Sleeplessness left me useless and severely tired every morning as I was slumped in my own spiritless world. I became unresponsive to Joy's company and to the presence of Jared.

I was introduced to sleeping pills to help induce my sleep at night, but it only left me unfocused and in a "funk" the next afternoon. The pills were slowly becoming a habitual crutch. My desperation blinded me from seeing how they were now depression's greatest friend disguised to trigger a repetitious cycle of hopelessness and despair. Phone calls from friends couldn't break me out of its spell. I refused to read the Bible. I turned away from worshipping to songs that once lifted my spirits.

In this season of depression, I learned something about the enemy's schemes: when you are vulnerable to depression, he will raise questions that seem to make sense, not unlike what he raised with Jesus in the wilderness. In Matthew 4, Jesus had just fasted 40 days; He was hungry and vulnerable. Listen to the devil's temptations:

> *"If you are the Son of God, tell these stones to become bread"* (Matthew 4:3 NIV).
>
> *"If you are the Son of God, throw yourself down . . . [and the angels] will lift you up in their hands"* (Matthew 4:6 NIV).
>
> *"All this I will give you, if you will bow down and worship me"* (Matthew 4:9 NIV)

Every question or challenge seemed to make sense. Jesus was the Son of God and could indeed turn the stones into bread. The angels would certainly lift Him up to prevent Jesus from being harmed. It all seemed to make sense.

In similar ways, in the vulnerable state of my mind, I was challenged by the voice of the enemy:

- "Perhaps it's time for you to give up the ministry."
- "If you're such a great spiritual leader, then why is the church doing good while you're absent?"
- "Maybe it's time to turn the church over to your son and you step away from the church and ministry."
- "Maybe your time is up."

Each question made sense, when considered in light of what I was experiencing. That's when the Lord responded: "Physical illness I can heal. But spiritual illness you must choose to reach out to Me, as the women who had been hemorrhaging reached out to touch the hem of My garment and was cured that moment (Luke 8:44*).*"

Depression is a dirty word, but healing is possible only if we choose to identify it for what it really is. Joy challenged me to pray for healing.

"I did," I said.

"What are you praying for?" she asked.

"That I will have the strength to break out of this depression, to fight against it so I'm not overcome by it anymore," I replied.

Then Joy confronted me with the crux of my condition: "Whose battle is it?"

"The battle is the Lord's," I said.

"Then, if the battle is the Lord's, why are you still hanging on to it? Why not pray that we give this depression to Him, let HIM fight it? For isn't it true that we battle not against flesh and blood, but against the spiritual forces of evil in the heavenly realms?"

Who was the real pastor here? Joy's challenge came directly from Ephesians 6:12:

> *"For our struggle is not against flesh and blood, but against the rulers, against the authorities, against the powers of this dark world and against the spiritual forces of evil in the heavenly realms."*

Joy pulled my hands toward her and we prayed and earnestly submitted all of what I was feeling to the Lord. We declared that every bit of what had been haunting me would be released to the Lord's care. I refused to hold onto anything, except to grasp the edge of His garment.

That night, I took my sleeping pill and cut it in half. The next night, I split the remaining half. Two nights later, I split it again that left me with just a tiny speck to take. Finally, after a week, no more sleeping pills!! Today, I sleep sounder than ever. I've often joked with Joy that I'm in such a deep sleep every night that the house could burn down and I wouldn't know it.

Don't allow your circumstances to guide your emotions. Instead, allow it to act as a gauge of your trust in Jesus. Sometimes we believe that a change in our circumstance will change our emotions;

- "If only I had a new job, I'd have less stress;" or,
- "If only he hadn't said that to me, I wouldn't be so angry today;" or,
- "If only I didn't marry him, I'd be happier today;" or,
- "If only God would heal me, then I can trust Him more."

When our focus rests on our circumstances or on other people as the cause for the way we feel, we allow it to dictate the path we will eventually take. In doing so, we trust in our circumstances to determine our emotions more than we do in our own responsibility to control it. Ultimately, what does this have to say about our trust in God?

When your circumstances seem stacked against you and you feel your emotions beginning to run away don't stare at the premises. Stand on His promises. Rather than allow your emotions to guide your actions, let it be a gauge of your trust in God. "Taking every thought captive to be obedient to Christ" (2 Corinthians 10:4 NIV) is not about who you think you are; it's about trusting in obedience to Christ to whom you belong and what God has already promised.

> *"Be strong and courageous. Do not be afraid; do not be discouraged, for the Lord your God will be with you wherever you go"* (Joshua 1:9 NIV).
>
> *"If God is for us, who can be against us?"* (Romans 8:31 NIV). *"Do not be anxious about anything, but in every situation, by prayer and petition, with thanksgiving, present your requests to God. And the peace of God, which transcends all understanding, will guard your hearts and your minds in Christ Jesus"* (Philippians 4:6 NIV).
>
> *"I can do all things through Him who strengthens me"* (Philippians 4:13 NIV).
>
> *"For you created my inmost being; you knit me together in my mother's womb. I praise you because I am fearfully and wonderfully made; your works are wonderful"* (Psalm 139:13-14 NIV).

When your true identity is grounded in Jesus Christ, you are no longer bound to your own feelings. The devil would love nothing better than to manipulate your circumstances into negative thoughts that will turn you away from Jesus and His promises. But God will *"turn all things for the good of those who love Him"* (Romans 8:28 NIV).

He will use your circumstances not to guide your emotions, but each challenge you encounter becomes a gauge to remind you that you can trust Him because of who you really are to Him – a child who is loved beyond comprehension; a child who is yet to receive His best; a child who He died for so that we might live. God doesn't see us for who we are or what we've done; He sees us for who we can become – a new creation in Jesus Christ.

Best way to defeat depression: focus on His promises, not your premises. Remember to whom you belong, not how you feel.

> *"I have been crucified with Christ and I no longer live, but Christ lives in me. The life I now live in the body, I live by faith in the Son of God, who loved me and gave himself for me"* (Galatians 2:20 NIV).

Fighting for Faith

"I have fought the good fight, I have finished the race, I have kept the faith."
(2 Timothy 4:7 NIV)

I received one of the most precious gifts to commemorate my journey: boxing gloves! Real and authentic, 100 percent leather boxing gloves. It was a gift I received straight from the heart of my sons, a treasured prize, not for what it could be use for (I've hidden them from Joy so she can't use it on me), but priceless for what it portrayed.

It would be an understatement to say that our family had been through a lot. Our world was shifted and turned upside down and inside out in just a matter of hours. The strain seemed unbearable at times. Hope faded as death attempted to steal my life.

As the battle raged on, however, my kids saw a fighter in me – someone who wasn’t willing to give up, nor give in. They saw a spirit within me that was trained to fight, regardless of the price demanded. They saw me suffer and watched my countenance dwindle, but they never saw me quit. And so, to commemorate our church's One-year Anniversary, they presented me with a symbol of that fighting spirit – a pair of boxing gloves!

The greatest battle that we will encounter in our lifetime is a challenge to our faith. Life is unfair and cruel, and sometimes, I wonder if it's only goal is to push us to the quitting point of our faith. As long as we exist in this world, our faith will be challenged. We’ll be challenged on different fronts: from within our families, from failed finances or wrapped in an unexpected diagnosis to our health. At what point will we quit and allow our frustrations and doubts to defeat us? Listen to what Paul wrote to his protégé, Timothy, as he prepared him for his own ministry journey:

> *"I have fought the good fight, I have finished the race, I have kept the faith. Now there is in store for me the crown of righteousness, which the Lord, the righteous Judge, will award to me on that day – and not only to me, but also to all who have longed for his appearing"* (2 Timothy 4:7-8 NIV).

Paul was threatened in many ways: persecuted and beaten, falsely accused and imprisoned, shipwrecked, and other near-death encounters. But regardless of the trial that tested his faith, Paul fought the "good fight;" i.e., he never gave up on his faith. Paul never quit. Regardless what he faced on his earthly journey, Jesus remained his Lord. Suffering was just another mile marker on his road to receive the crown of righteousness that awaited the faithful willing to fight and not resign.

My journey continues. I don't believe God is finished with me yet. My suffering was a necessary challenge to my faith that pressed me to reveal my quitting point. Jesus was pressed in the Garden; Paul was challenged on the road to Rome; I was crushed in the valley of the shadow of death. But my faith remains.

Boxing gloves . . . in heaven there must be a wall full of them hanging and labeled with the names of God's faithful. Lord, when my time is up, may my pair of gloves be added to Your wall of faith.

Stepping Into the Miraculous

"I will never be the same again.
I can never return, I've closed the door."
Darlene Zschech

It was in the 1990s that Hillsong, an Australian worship group led by songwriter, Darlene Zschech, introduced her classic to the world that speaks of a life that has been changed and transformed by a miraculous God. When we've been touched by the hand of God, like Jacob when he wrestled with God, our lives can never be the same again. Here's an excerpt:

> *"I will never be the same again,*
> *I can never return, I've closed the door.*
> *I will walk the path, I'll run the race*
> *And I will never be the same again.*
> . . .
> *There are higher heights, there are deeper seas,*
> *Whatever you need to do, Lord do in me.*
> *The Glory of God fills my life,*
> *And I will never be the same again."*

Somehow once you've stepped into the miraculous, and the "glory of God" has filled your life, you will never be the same. That was certainly the case with the leper Jesus healed in Mark 1; and blind Bartimaeus in Mark 10, and others who experienced the supremacy of an all-powerful God. To the healed paralytic, and the woman healed from hemorrhaging, "normalcy" took on a different meaning. Their experience took them to a deeper depth with Jesus allowing them to see life through the eyes of the Father, open and willing to do whatever the Father required of them. They could never be the same again.

We received the pathologist's report of my second bone marrow biopsy. Results: **NO "abnormal cells"** present; analysis **negative** for leukemic cells!! To this I shout "Hallelujah" to my God and King! From an initial report of being 95 percent leukemic to a report that I was now leukemic free, I counted as a miracle! As my doctor explained the results, and after two years of follow-ups, blood tests, needle pokes, transfusions and examinations, he finally pronounced me "healed."

Surprised to hear his prognosis, I questioned him just to make sure, "It's usually "remission," isn't it?"

But, once again he reassured me, I was healed! No more medications, no more intrusive needles, no more chemotherapy, no more doctor visits. It had finally come to an end. I was overwhelmed by emotions.

"Thank you, thank you, thank you," I whispered to him. "How can I ever repay you?"

To which, my doctor, a man of few words said, "Live." It was short, but profound.

It all made sense now. Under the shadows of suffering, God calls upon us to trust, to hope, to believe in the miraculous and LIVE! Having just stepped into the miraculous, how can my life ever be the same again? To our family, our friends and everyone who experienced this incredible journey with us, never forget the miraculous that we witnessed. God is real and He reigns! We will never be the same again.

Father, thank You for Your faithfulness that allowed me to suffer for the sake of bringing credibility to Your Gospel. Forgive me for struggling to see beyond my own suffering and failing to see each step that was used to bring me closer to the miraculous You were about to reveal in my life. My journey continues. I now travel with a deeper reverence for You and a reaffirmation of the miraculous power with which You reign. I stand in awe of Your faithfulness towards us. I will never be the same again.

Epilogue

"I thank my God every time I remember you.
In all my prayers for all of you, I always pray with joy because of your partnership in the gospel from the first day until now, being confident of this, that he who began a good work in you will carry it on to completion until the day of Christ Jesus."
(Philippians 1:3-6 NIV)

Life is full of the unexpected; it's what we all face, every day. It's what we choose to do with the unfulfilled anticipations, broken promises, even unanswered prayers that send you to the trashcan of rejection that makes all the difference in the world.

Here's a spiritual principle I learned a long time ago: "When life gives you lemons, make lemonade." All right, I confess that you won't find this direct quote anywhere in the Bible. What you will find, however, are references to the Father's heart on how we should choose to live, despite the "lemons" we encounter along the way:

> *"A righteous man falls seven times, but rises again"* (Proverbs 24:16 NIV).

> *"Love your enemies, bless those who curse you, do good to those who hate you, and pray for those who spitefully use you and persecute you that you may be sons of your Father in heaven"* (Matthew 5:44 NIV).

> *"For whoever wants to save his life will lose it, but whoever loses his life for me will save it"* (Luke 9:24 NIV).

> *"Rejoice in the Lord always. I will say it again, Rejoice!"* (Philippians 4:4 NIV).

When life's unexpected hits you square in the face and knocks you down, stand up, love, bless, do good, pray, lose your own life for another and rejoice in Him . . . always.

So, is it really enough that "when life gives you lemons, you make lemonade?" I think we do a disservice to the underlying heart of the Father by simply making just lemonade. Why stop there? Why not turn lemons into velvety lemon meringue pie lemon chiffon cake, lemon curd with chocolate chip and cream cheese scones, or sautéed Onaga (long tailed red snapper) with lemon-butter, capers and white wine sauce, or sweet-sour lemon glazed chicken ... you get the picture.

Life will toss the unexpected at us. Our role: make lemonade and more, even beyond what life was expecting in return. So, rather than reject the unexpected, receive it and squeeze every bit of good you can from it, and in Jesus' Name, rejoice and live out His promises! After all, perhaps the miraculous begins with the Hope we'll find in one squeezed lemon at a time. Perhaps the miracles are discovered in what you choose to make of the journey God places in front of you. My prayer for you is that you find hope, healing and the miraculous on your journey with God. And when you do, LIVE!

"Let your hopes, not your hurts, shape your future."
(Robert H. Schuller)

"We must accept finite disappointment,
but never lose infinite hope."
(Dr. Martin Luther King, Jr.)

One last thing before you go. If you've found this book to be helpful to you, would you kindly recommend it to someone who will also benefit from it? You may also go to Amazon.com to locate additional copies of this book and write a review of it so others may find hope when the unexpected strikes at their lives.

For more information, log on to www.elwinahu.com.

"May the God of hope fill you with all joy and peace as you trust in Him, so that you may overflow with hope by the power of the Holy Spirit."
(Romans 15:13 NIV)

Made in the USA
San Bernardino, CA
07 March 2017